ENGAGING
LEARNERS
EVERYWHERE

ENGAGING LEARNERS EVERYWHERE

The Interactive Synchronous HyFlex Method

NATHAN MENTZER
ABDUL MOEED ASAD
ADRIE A. KOEHLER
LAKSHMY MOHANDAS
ELNARA MAMMADOVA

Purdue University Press
West Lafayette, Indiana

Copyright © 2025 by Nathan Mentzer, Adrie Koehler, Lakshmy Mohandas, Abdul Moeed Asad, and Elnara Mammadova. All rights reserved.
Cataloging-in-Publication Data is on file at the Library of Congress.

978-1-62671-228-7 (PPB)
978-1-62671-216-4 (epdf)
9781-6-2671-181-5 (epub)

Cover image by Abdul Moeed Asad

CONTENTS

Preface   xi

Acknowledgments   xv

How to Use This Book   xvi
   What's Inside?   xviii
   Key Questions and Considerations   xix
      Before Class: Setting the Stage   xix
      During Class: Facilitating Engaging and Inclusive Sessions   xx
      After Class: Reflecting and Refining Your Approach   xx

1   Introduction to Interactive Synchronous HyFlex   1
   What Is Interactive Synchronous HyFlex?   1
   The Context and Potential for Transfer of Interactive Synchronous HyFlex from Our Context to Yours   3
   Why Consider Implementing HyFlex Classrooms?   4
      HyFlex Offers Flexibility That Makes Classrooms Robust   5
      The Use of Technology Enables New Capabilities   6
         Videoconferencing Software Enables More Accessible Classrooms   6
         Embracing Affordances of Digital Artifacts in Interactive Synchronous HyFlex   8
   The Costs of Implementing Interactive Synchronous HyFlex   9
      Technological Complexity   9
         Teacher Perspective   9
         Student Perspective   10
      Cognitive Complexity   11
         Teacher Perspective   11
         Student Perspective   11
      Planning   11
         Teacher Perspective   11
         Student Perspective   12

Design Principles of the Interactive Synchronous HyFlex Model	12
1. Low Overhead: Getting Started Is Easy	13
2. Student Autonomy: More Robust Attendance	15
3. Accessibility: More Ways to Engage	15
Community of Inquiry (CoI)	18
Social Presence	18
Cognitive Presence	19
Teaching Presence	19
Final Words on Considering Interactive Synchronous HyFlex	20
References	20

2   Transitioning to an Interactive Synchronous HyFlex Classroom   21

Part 1: Setting Expectations	22
How Flexible Should Your HyFlex Course Be?	22
Anticipating Challenges	24
Who Gets to Be Remote (and for How Long)?	25
Remote Students: Are They Engaged?	26
Are Remote Students Getting the Support They Need?	27
Are Face-to-Face Students Getting the Support They Need?	29
Example Expectations	29
Developing Expectations for Meaningful Interactions	31
Part 2: Setting Up the Classroom Environment for Interactive Synchronous HyFlex	35
How to Configure Your LMS to Support Interactive Synchronous HyFlex Environments	36
Inclusive of All (Remote and Face-to-Face) Students	36
Easy to Access	37
Important Resources	37
How to Set Up and Use Your Collaboration Software	39
Special Purpose Channels	40
Session-Specific Channels	40
Small Group Channels	40
Part 3: Preparing Classroom Activities for HyFlex	43
Instructional Approach	43
Instruction	45

	General Activities	45
	Team-Based Activities	46
	Support	47
	References	48
3	**Facilitating Interactive Synchronous HyFlex Classrooms**	49
	Part 1: Final Preparations for The Semester	50
	Ensuring a Smooth Start	50
	Practice Builds Confidence and Competence	53
	Mechanical Tasks	54
	Engagement Tasks	54
	Part 2: Navigating The First Days of Class	55
	1. Establish Your Presence to Build Rapport and Model Behavior	56
	2. Fostering Community Across Modalities	58
	3. Think About Accessibility	58
	Part 3: Maintaining Daily Interactions	60
	Kicking Off Class	60
	During Class Facilitation	61
	Toolkit for Troubleshooting	61
	Part 4: Supporting Students After Class	62
	Support Resources	62
	Classroom Recordings	62
	Methods of Communication	62
	References	63
4	**HyFlex Vignettes**	64
	Vignettes	65
	Vignette 1: EDCI 558, Methods of Teaching Integrated STEM (Secondary Education)	65
	Vignette 2: TLI 361, Engineering and Technology Education Instructional Planning and Evaluation; and TLI 262, Foundations of Integrated STEM Education	68
	Vignette 3: EDCI 490, Engineering by Design—Elementary	70
	Vignette 4: EPICS HyFlex Course, Bridging Campuses for Student-Led Community Impact	72

5   A Synopsis of Interactive Synchronous HyFlex Research   77

Studies   79

    Study 1: Mohandas, Lakshmy. 2022. "The Impact of Interactive Synchronous Hyflex Model on Students' Perception of Social, Teaching and Cognitive Presence in a Design Thinking Course." PhD diss., Purdue University   79

    Study 2: Mohandas, Lakshmy, Nathan Mentzer, Adrie Koehler, and Shawn Farrington. 2023. "To Be Face-to-Face Today or to Be Remote Today: That Is the Question." In *Proceedings of the 2023 AERA Annual Meeting*. AERA.   81

    Study 3: Mentzer, Nathan, and Lakshmy Mohandas. 2022. "Student Experiences in an Interactive Synchronous HyFlex Design Thinking Course During COVID-19." *Interactive Learning Environments* 32 (5): 1613–28.   82

    Study 4: Mentzer, Nathan, Bhawna Krishna, Ankita Kotangale, and Lakshmy Mohandas. 2023. "HyFlex Environment: Addressing Students' Basic Psychological Needs." *Learning Environments Research* 26 (1): 271–89.   84

    Study 5: Mentzer, Nathan J., Tonya M. Isabell, and Lakshmy Mohandas. 2024. "The Impact of Interactive Synchronous HyFlex Model on Student Academic Performance in a Large Active Learning Introductory College Design Course." *Journal of Computing in Higher Education* 36 (3): 619–46.   86

    Study 6: Mentzer, Nathan, Shawn Farrington, Jenica Woolley, and Lakshmy Mohandas. 2025. "Deep Learning." Unpublished work, currently in progress.   88

    Study 7: Mohandas, Lakshmy, Nathan Mentzer, Adrie Koehler, Shawn Farrington, and Elnara Mammadova. 2023. "Understanding Students' Self-Regulation in a HyFlex Design Thinking Course." *2023 ASEE Annual Conference & Exposition*.   90

    Study 8: Krishna, Bhawna. 2023. "Effect of Modalities on Group Performance in HyFlex Environment." Master's thesis, Purdue University.   92

    Study 9: Mentzer, Nathan, Elnara Mammadova, Adrie Koehler, Lakshmy Mohandas, and Shawn Farrington. 2025. "Analyzing the Impact of Basic Psychological Needs on Student Academic Performance: A Comparison of Post-Pandemic Interactive Synchronous Hyflex and Pre-Pandemic Traditional Face-to-Face Instruction." *Educational Technology Research and Development* 73 (1): 91–114. https://doi.org/10.1007/s11423-024-10417-2.   94

Study 10: Koehler, Adrie, Lakshmy Mohandas, Nathan Mentzer, and Elnara Mammadova. 2025. "Teaching Across Modalities: HyFlex Instructor Presence." Manuscript under review. 98
Study 11: "Onboarding to HyFlex as a New Instructor." Unpublished work, currently in progress. 100
Study 12: Mammadova, Elnara, Nathan Mentzer, and Emre Topalgokceli. 2025. "Impact of Disability Accommodations on Learning Experiences Among Undergraduate Students in HyFlex." Paper presented at the American Educational Research Association Annual Meeting, Denver, CO, April. 103

Summary of the Articles 106
   Expectations and Messaging 106
   Course Design and Facilitation 107
   Technology-Mediated Interactions 108

Implications 109

References 109

6 Troubleshooting and Improving Your Interactive Synchronous HyFlex Instruction   114

Part 1: What to Do When You Run into Difficulty 114
   Communicate with Your Students 116
   Renew (Inclusive) Norms 116
   Ask for Help 117

Part 2: Improving Your HyFlex Instructional Practice 118
   Use Recordings to Your Advantage 118
   Observe Other HyFlex Instructors 119
   Ask Your Students 119
   Ask for a Second Opinion 119
   Experiment! 120

Conclusion 121
   Key Takeaways 121
      Setting Clear Expectations 121
      Establish an Inclusive and Engaging Culture 122
      Leverage Technologies That Facilitate Interaction Across Modalities 123
      Keep On Improving 124
   Final Thoughts 124
   References 125

PREFACE

In early 2020, few could foresee the drastic transformation awaiting education. I recall listening to NPR sharing news of a virus abroad while driving my kids to early morning swim practice in January and February. As a professor at Purdue University, one of my responsibilities was to facilitate the implementation of a large required first-year course on design thinking. This course hinges on student interaction where teams of students work together to develop solutions to real-world problems. As news of the virus spread, I began to wonder: *What might campus look like if some students return after spring break and bring the virus back to campus? What if travel restrictions keep some students away? What if campus closed for a period of time?* While student attendance is an enduring concern, anticipating the sheer magnitude of students unable to attend class during the pandemic forced us to rethink how to make classes accessible. This book shares the lessons we learned and why they matter going forward. It is not just about crisis response. It is about reimagining classrooms to serve the needs of students—whoever and wherever they are.

At about 9 a.m. on Friday, March 6, 2020, six business days prior to spring break, our department head casually spent a few minutes introducing the faculty to Microsoft Teams, "just in case" we needed to use it. I had heard of the software before, but that was the first time I thought about it as a tool we might need to use. It looked a little like Zoom or Google Hangouts, but the log-in was seamlessly integrated into our campus log-in system, the interface supported student autonomy, and it had a durable ecosystem that was available, like an unlocked physical workspace, before and after meetings. Just a few hours after our meeting, we realized we could implement Microsoft Teams in our classroom prior to break so that if it were needed afterward (perhaps campus was closed for a few days or student absences were disruptive), we'd be familiar and ready. For context, up to that point most veteran instructors could only remember campus being closed for ice one day during their tenure—campus closure was practically unheard of.

Using Microsoft Teams, we created two teams, one for each classroom, and we named them with the room numbers so students could go to Knoy B16 or B19 either face-to-face or remotely. Monday, March 9, started normally and instructors introduced the software and procedure. All students joined their Microsoft Teams team from the classroom and experimented with the software using their laptops or phones. At first the audio was a disaster, with microphones and speakers from forty students squealing with feedback in section after section. However, within a few days, the students and instructors began to figure out how to join the team quickly and to mute and unmute at appropriate times. By Friday, March 13, the COVID-19 virus had spread quickly in the US and, as a result, only a few students continued face-to-face attendance as the rest left campus early and transitioned to remote participation in our course. And with that, our HyFlex model was born. Most importantly, that week, the lesson we learned was that learning was not limited to those in physical attendance.

Purdue, like many other institutions, pivoted to a fully remote approach after spring break and we were already prepared for it. Students knew how to log on to Microsoft Teams and they had already navigated the security settings to allow video, audio, and screen sharing. As a result of this structure and preparation, class resumed remotely and relatively smoothly for our course sections. Our most significant hurdles were the varied time zones and internet bandwidth associated with students' remote locations. We moved some students to sections that met later (or earlier) in the day to better synchronize with their home time zone, and we encouraged, but did not require, students to use their cameras. Students connected from home, internet cafes, hospitals, and quarantine facilities throughout the world. In a time of worldwide social isolation, our class was synchronous, interactive, and, according to students, the only time in their week when they had meaningful academic work in collaboration with their peers.

In July of 2020, Purdue was among the first to resume face-to-face classes in the COVID-19 era, and we felt as ready as we could be. We took what we had learned during the blended week prior to spring break and the fully remote months that followed and created a face-to-face version of our course that facilitated synchronous remote participation as needed. The foundation of our HyFlex course was sturdy and functional, and the details of communicating expectations with students and fostering connectivity evolved with practice.

Our success in the spring and summer of 2020 started the evolution of what we now fondly call "Interactive Synchronous HyFlex." Our development and research were initially funded by a Best Practices in Higher Education grant from the Provost's office, which led to another grant from the National Science Foundation. Now, based on nearly five years of fall, spring, and summer implementations, this book shares our recipe for a successful interactive and synchronous

HyFlex learning environment. Over the semesters since spring 2020, with each iteration we made small improvements to optimize the experience for students and their instructors. We have presented and published our work, critically analyzing student and instructor experiences. This e-book complements our existing research-based discoveries by sharing our pedagogical decisions and rationale. Unlike a traditional recipe, in the pages that follow we focus on the *how* and *why* as opposed to a brief list of the ingredients. In the following chapters we frame our approach in terms of our goals, our frameworks, and the questions we ask ourselves. We share answers to our questions as *a* model, not *the* model, but *a* model that fits a specific use case where our learning environment is active and interactive such that students work primarily in teams interacting with each other and their instructor. We recognize the delicate dance between instructional design as a creative work and instructional technology as a tool with affordances and limitations. We also acknowledge that our use of instructional technology will become dated as the technology changes; however, we anticipate that readers will see past the button clicks and gain insights from our approach to HyFlex as a pedagogy in pursuit of accessibility.

—Nathan Mentzer, PhD

ACKNOWLEDGMENTS

Abdul Moeed Asad is a gifted storyteller. Moeed joined the instructional team as a graduate student in 2022, after the HyFlex model had begun to solidify. He embraced the approach and forged his own HyFlex personality naturally by learning from our past and experimenting in his classroom. Moeed was a peer to other graduate students and a respected emerging leader. He joined every weekly instructional planning meeting with a smile. As our HyFlex approach formalized, Moeed took the lead at telling our story through this book. He reflected on the team's collective efforts in teaching to organize the chapters, drafted chapters for feedback from the research team, and envisioned formatting to enhance the reader's experience. Beyond the writing, he has collected quotes, sketched illustrations, and taken photos to bring this book to life. While Dr. Nathan Mentzer is the first author of this final product of the grant he led, Moeed is to be recognized as *the storyteller* of our collective HyFlex story.

This text is based on discoveries made possible by the National Science Foundation Grant Number 2110799 led by Dr. Nathan Mentzer and the efforts of a team of co-principal investigators: Dr. Adrie Koehler, Dr. Lakshmy Mohandas, and Shawn Farrington.

Our work is informed by an advisory board and external evaluators rich with experience and insights. The advisory board, which has met annually to guide the project and provided peer review for this text, is composed of Dr. Jenna Rickus, senior vice provost for teaching and learning at Purdue University; Dr. Chantal Levesque-Bristol, executive director of the Purdue University Center for Instructional Excellence; Dr. Annelies Raes, assistant professor in instructional psychology and technology at the University of Leuven, Belgium, and invited professor at the University of Lille, France; Dr. Fien Depaepe, professor of psychology and educational sciences in the Center for Instructional Psychology and Technology at the University of Leuven, Belgium; and Dr. Brian Beatty, professor of instructional technologies in the Department of Equity, Leadership Studies, and Instructional Technologies at San Francisco State University. Michelle Phillips and associates Jen Helms and Laurie Lopez provided external evaluation and formative feedback throughout the project.

HOW TO USE THIS BOOK

Across its six chapters, this book is meant to be a guide to support instructors as they

1. gain awareness of the opportunities to make courses more accessible by using the Interactive Synchronous HyFlex model (chapter 1);
2. understand what it takes to design (chapter 2) and implement (chapters 2 and 3) our research (chapter 5)-based model;
3. gain inspiration on how Interactive Synchronous HyFlex principles can transfer to their context (chapter 4); and
4. troubleshoot challenges of the Interactive Synchronous HyFlex classroom (chapter 6).

Although this book was written in the context of problem-based team environments for undergraduate students, many of the insights shared here are likely transferable to other contexts. We have aimed for accessibility in our explanations but also provided references to our research (see chapter 5) where appropriate for those who may wish to dive deeper into the evidence behind our recommendations. As an example, in recent years, like higher education, K–12 education has become an experience occurring across face-to-face, blended, and online environments. While K–12 comes with unique constraints and considerations, the foundational elements for creating an interactive blended learning experience are articulated in this book, offering K–12 educators insight into how to get started, questions to consider throughout the process, and examples of how the process can be completed in a specific context. In short, this book serves as a design case for designing and implementing problem-based learning in blended environments. By telling our design story, we are hopeful that others can use it to inform their design choices, as they design, implement, and facilitate problem-based blended learning experiences.

Imagine a technology instructional specialist who is responsible for preparing all teachers in a K–12 school corporation to create meaningful learning experiences as part of a new HyFlex initiative the school is offering. Although she is well-versed in using technology, is a former high school teacher, has taught in both face-to-face and online settings, and has prepared many professional development trainings for teachers, she has limited experience with designing and teaching in HyFlex learning environments. Her administration is pushing for all teachers across the corporation to create more accessible learning experiences, and many of the teachers are reluctant to embrace HyFlex as a learning option because they have fears related to student participation and workload requirements.

As she considers her options for learning more about HyFlex learning, she comes across *Engaging Learners Everywhere: The Interactive Synchronous HyFlex Method*. While initially she is uncertain about whether a book focused on the experiences of designing and implementing HyFlex for an undergraduate audience would be beneficial for her, she realizes that the book can help guide how she thinks about HyFlex and key decision-making points. While she realizes that K–12 students are different from the audience discussed in the book in many ways (e.g., autonomy, needs, levels), she starts to see the design process used for creating HyFlex learning and how she can use it to design something that is appropriate for her context.

Although she has located limited research and concrete examples of using HyFlex in K–12 settings, she envisions multiple ways that this approach might elevate teachers' practice in her corporation. For instance, in elementary classrooms, parents play a critical role in supporting students' success. She sees how teachers can use HyFlex to connect parents with what is happening in the classroom (e.g., how to work math problems) or to support parents to help their children catch up after missing school due to illness. At the same time, with high school students, she sees that teachers can use HyFlex to bring students synchronously into the classroom if they are physically unable to be there or bring the classroom to them asynchronously if they are ill. Across all levels, she envisions HyFlex creating opportunities for offering individualized support for missed lessons, remediation, or enrichment.

WHAT'S INSIDE?

This book contains six chapters: four are instructional (chapters 1, 2, 3, and 6) and two have a special purpose (chapters 4 and 5). The instructional chapters guide educators through implementing the Interactive Synchronous HyFlex model, from understanding its benefits and costs (chapter 1) to planning (chapter 2), day-to-day facilitation (chapter 3), and troubleshooting challenges (chapter 6). The special chapters present vignettes with visuals to inspire transfer to a broad range of classrooms (chapter 4) and summarize our research, equipping readers with evidence to support their own decision-making (chapter 5). Finally, the conclusion distills key takeaways from the book.

KEY QUESTIONS AND CONSIDERATIONS

To help you navigate this book effectively, following are some key questions and considerations discussed in the instructional chapters, along with where to find their answers.

BEFORE CLASS: SETTING THE STAGE

- **What is Interactive Synchronous HyFlex and why should I consider it?** Interactive Synchronous HyFlex offers flexibility for students to engage remotely or face-to-face, making classrooms more robust and accessible. See chapter 1, "Introduction to Interactive Synchronous HyFlex," for a detailed explanation of its description, benefits, and the technology it utilizes.
- **How flexible should my HyFlex course be?** Determine the degree of flexibility suitable for your course, considering factors like student autonomy, equity, course goals, and desired classroom culture. Explore chapter 2, "Transitioning to an Interactive Synchronous HyFlex Classroom," for guidance on setting expectations and addressing potential challenges.
- **How do I prepare my classroom environment for HyFlex?** Create a supportive remote infrastructure using your learning management system and collaboration software (e.g., Microsoft Teams). Chapter 2 provides detailed instructions on configuring your LMS for access to resources, setting up communication channels in your collaboration software, and establishing clear expectations for engagement.
- **How do I prepare classroom activities for HyFlex?** Adapt your teaching materials and activities to engage both remote and face-to-face students. Chapter 2 offers insights into structuring your course, utilizing technology effectively, and fostering inclusive participation.
- **How can I ensure a smooth start to my HyFlex class?** Chapter 3, "Facilitating Interactive Synchronous HyFlex Classrooms," outlines essential

steps to prepare before the first day, including setting up technology, communicating expectations, and practicing for confidence.

DURING CLASS:
FACILITATING ENGAGING AND INCLUSIVE SESSIONS

- **How do I establish my presence and build rapport in a HyFlex classroom?** Project a welcoming demeanor, engage students across modalities, and model effective HyFlex interactions. Chapter 3 provides practical tips for building community and ensuring accessibility for all.
- **How do I support students in a HyFlex environment?** Encourage active participation, address technical issues, monitor group dynamics, and be available for questions. Chapter 3 offers strategies for maintaining a positive and inclusive learning environment.

AFTER CLASS:
REFLECTING AND REFINING YOUR APPROACH

- **What can I do when I encounter difficulties in my HyFlex classroom?** Communicate openly with students, reiterate expectations, model inclusive behaviors, and seek support from colleagues or remote communities. Refer to chapter 6, "Troubleshooting and Improving Your Interactive Synchronous HyFlex Instruction," for detailed guidance.
- **How can I improve my HyFlex instructional practice?** Chapter 6 emphasizes the importance of self-reflection, observing experienced colleagues, and seeking external feedback. Embrace a mindset of continuous improvement to refine your HyFlex teaching.

1

INTRODUCTION TO INTERACTIVE SYNCHRONOUS HYFLEX

In this book, we share lessons learned from our research-based teaching practice on how we adapted HyFlex to fit our specific needs for a hands-on, student-centered, team-based context in higher education. HyFlex, or Hybrid-Flexible, is a portmanteau coined by Dr. Brian Beatty (Beatty 2019) developed to accommodate students who could not consistently attend face-to-face classes. Our adapted model is called *Interactive Synchronous HyFlex* and it is a course design and teaching approach that affords robust and accessible attendance for students.

WHAT IS INTERACTIVE SYNCHRONOUS HYFLEX?

The Interactive Synchronous HyFlex model allows students to choose the modality that best suits them on any given day, granting them the freedom to join class either remotely or face-to-face. Through this approach, a typical class session simultaneously accommodates both face-to-face and remote students synchronously working together during their assigned class time as shown in figure 1.1.

FIGURE 1.1 (*Left*) In interactive synchronous HyFlex, students can participate remotely or face-to-face during a class session. (*Right*) In interactive synchronous HyFlex, students can participate remotely or face-to-face during a class session. SOURCE: Abdul Moeed Asad (Co-author)

WHAT THE TERM INTERACTIVE SYNCHRONOUS HYFLEX MEANS	
INTERACTIVE	Emphasizes real-time collaboration during active learning activities in a problem-based course, where students can participate equally regardless of their mode of attendance.
SYNCHRONOUS	Requires students to participate in real time, attending class either remotely or face-to-face at a designated class time.
HYFLEX	Emphasizes students' flexibility (hence the "flex-ible" from HyFlex) to join either remotely or face-to-face with equal opportunity to learn regardless of their mode of attendance. The decision to be remote or face-to-face can be made on a per session basis.

Students come to class expecting to work in blended groups (groups with both remote and face-to-face students) to complete team-based activities, such as drawing affinity maps, whiteboarding ideas, and building solutions. We call our specific version of HyFlex *Interactive Synchronous* because of its emphasis on real-time collaboration during an active learning, problem-based course.

We believe HyFlex classrooms are fundamentally more robust and equitable classroom environments compared with traditional classrooms, and in the section "Why Consider Implementing HyFlex Classrooms?" later in this chapter we discuss why you might consider offering your course using this modality.

| FURTHER READING  | Asynchronous HyFlex

Synchronous HyFlex is great for traditional classrooms. However, there are instances of HyFlex that operate primarily in an asynchronous mode. If you'd like to explore asynchronous modes, a good place to start is Dr. Brain Beatty's work (see https://edtechbooks.org/hyflex/teaching_hyflex). |
|---|---|
| RESEARCH SPOTLIGHT  | Our Work Started Out from Necessity During COVID-19

Refer to Study 3 (chapter 5) for insights into how students experienced the Interactive Synchronous HyFlex model during the COVID-19 pandemic. |

THE CONTEXT AND POTENTIAL FOR TRANSFER OF INTERACTIVE SYNCHRONOUS HYFLEX FROM OUR CONTEXT TO YOURS

This text is based on our research and experience teaching an introductory design course for undergraduate students in multiple sections during the fall, spring, and summer terms across five years (2020–2025). With over twelve hundred students enrolling in the course each year, each section has approximately forty students. Students are supported by an instructor and an undergraduate teaching assistant. Each class typically starts with a short lecture to introduce concepts and prepare students for the session's activity. The class then transitions to team-based small groups, where students engage in problem-focused work toward ongoing projects.

The principles of Interactive Synchronous HyFlex therefore have proven to work in large group instruction and in team-based and problem-based contexts. We see its success at Purdue's Polytechnic Institute as a thoroughly tested case of its versatility: If it works for hundreds of students in a busy, active learning environment, it can likely fit the scale and style of your own teaching. Through sharing our approach, we hope you can use it to inform your course design decisions.

RESEARCH SPOTLIGHT 	**Does Participation Mode Affect Classroom Community?** *See chapter 5 for details.* Refer to Study 2 to understand how students perceived classroom communities across different participation modes in a HyFlex environment.

RESEARCH SPOTLIGHT 	**Can Interactive Synchronous HyFlex Improve Academic Performance?** *See chapter 5 for details.* Refer to Study 5 for an analysis of the impact of the Interactive Synchronous HyFlex model on student academic performance.

While the introductory design course serves as a context for this book, the co-authors have successfully experimented with Interactive Synchronous HyFlex in other courses, including graduate and undergraduate levels ranging from three to seventy students and taught by a single or multiple instructors (in one case, one co-instructor was permanently remote). Chapter 4 expands the conversation to include additional classes that have been taught using the HyFlex modality as contrasting cases. By sharing these cases, we aim to give you the confidence and clarity to incorporate the model into your own teaching environment.

WHY CONSIDER IMPLEMENTING HYFLEX CLASSROOMS?

While Interactive Synchronous HyFlex was initially born out of the necessity to make classrooms safe and accessible during the Covid-19 pandemic, its legacy continues to be transformative. In this section, we will see how Interactive Synchronous HyFlex goes beyond accommodating distance learning by opening the door to new capabilities in the classroom, allowing instructors to more easily support students' diverse needs and preferences.

HYFLEX OFFERS FLEXIBILITY THAT MAKES CLASSROOMS ROBUST

According to external evaluations of our program, students say the biggest benefit of Interactive Synchronous HyFlex is the freedom to attend class remotely or face-to-face. That flexibility keeps them engaged through bad weather—whether a snowstorm, monsoon shower, or heavy fog—mild sickness, or other competing priorities. In a traditional classroom, hazardous conditions often mean missed classes or even cancellations. However, with Interactive Synchronous HyFlex, a session can seamlessly shift online with little to no extra work for the instructor or students. Students already know where to find meeting links and how to participate remotely, so this switch between face-to-face and remote is smooth and keeps everyone on track.

FIGURE 1.2 Interactive Synchronous HyFlex enables robust attendance even in inclement weather. SOURCE: Zac Durant (Unsplash)

> *I tested for Covid recently and the result came back positive. [My supervisor] and I concluded it would be best for me to deliver the class remotely to avoid the possibility of spreading the virus inadvertently.*

> *The point I'd like to highlight here is the fact that students continue to work in groups on campus. [My supervisor] and I thought this would be the best way to ensure that the groups continue to work efficiently to successfully complete [the capstone project].*
>
> —GABRIEL RUIZ CASTRO, INSTRUCTOR 2023–2025

THE USE OF TECHNOLOGY ENABLES NEW CAPABILITIES

Interactive Synchronous HyFlex classrooms embrace technology to ensure effective and accessible collaboration between students. Here we will discuss how videoconferencing and other digital tools have become far more enabling for people with disabilities and how the embrace of technological tools has inherent benefits.

VIDEOCONFERENCING SOFTWARE ENABLES MORE ACCESSIBLE CLASSROOMS

Videoconferencing software, like Microsoft Teams, offers technological affordances that simultaneously benefit those attending the classroom while

FIGURE 1.3 Students can use live captions because of videoconferencing software, which we also call collaboration software. SOURCE: Abdul Moeed Asad (Co-author)

accommodating remote learners, which is a key principle of universal design for learning (UDL). Universal design for learning provides a foundation for pedagogy that focuses on benefits for all learners rather than prioritizing one learner group to the detriment of another (Beatty 2019). Here are some of the advantages of the inclusion of videoconferencing in the classroom:

- *Additional modes of participation:* The ability to communicate in multiple modes such as chat channels can encourage shy or introverted students to participate.
- *Easy content sharing:* Students sitting anywhere in the classroom can easily share files or use screen sharing to quickly share their or their group's work.
- *Enhanced screen access:* Students seated farther away from presentation displays in a physical classroom can use videoconferencing features for a better view.
- *Language accessibility:* Live auto-transcription in English makes the classroom more accessible to non-native speakers and d/Deaf and hard of hearing students, as well as those interpreting different accents in spoken English, by allowing them to follow alongside spoken words for better understanding (see figure 1.3).
- *Support for classroom transcription and recordings:* Students can review material later using classroom recordings (see figure 1.4) with features such as captioning and playback controls that facilitate comprehension, which meets the needs of a diverse range of students.

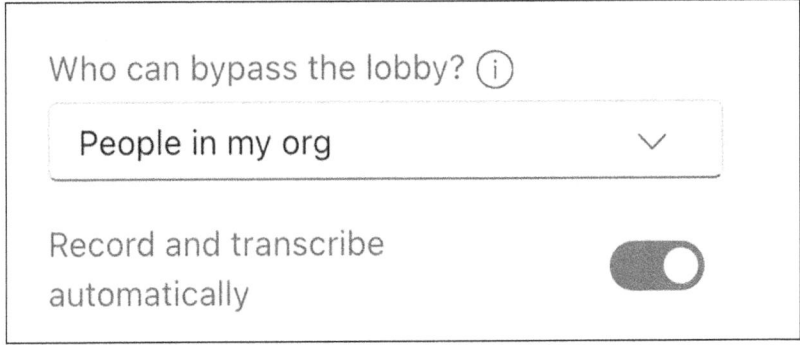

FIGURE 1.4 You can automatically record and transcribe meetings when you schedule a meeting on Microsoft Teams. The recorded meeting shows up as a mention on the thread. SOURCE: Screenshot of Microsoft Teams (Abdul Moeed Asad)

- *Bonus feature—reduced instructional effort to catch up students:* Easy transcription and recordings can accommodate students needing to miss class. Instructors can direct them to class recordings so that they can catch up on missed instruction (with a slightly modified assignment if needed).

> *What I found useful about Hyflex was being able to assist students who have to take leave, whether for personal reasons or Purdue-affiliated, and being able to easily guide them to refer to past recorded lectures.*
> —MAHAM GHAZANFAR, INSTRUCTOR 2022-2024

RESEARCH SPOTLIGHT

Does HyFlex Enhance Learning for Students with Disabilities?

See chapter 5 for details.

Refer to Study 12 to determine how HyFlex instruction impacts the learning and performance of students with disabilities compared with those without accommodations.

EMBRACING AFFORDANCES OF DIGITAL ARTIFACTS IN INTERACTIVE SYNCHRONOUS HYFLEX

In Interactive Synchronous HyFlex classrooms, we emphasize the use of digital documents (e.g., Google Docs), whiteboards (e.g., Miro), and discussion forums (e.g., channels in Microsoft Teams) over their physical counterparts. Not only are digital tools more inclusive for remote students because of their ability to allow for distributed work but they also offer the following multiple affordances that make them effective for work in general:

FIGURE 1.5 According to a McKinsey report (as cited in Valamis, 2019), employees spend hours every week searching and gathering information. Now imagine if you had to do all your searching without a search function. SOURCE: Abdul Moeed Asad (Co-author)

- *Permanence:* Digital artifacts allow for easy archiving and searching, mitigating some of the challenges shown in figure 1.5—that is, students can revisit feedback session artifacts (e.g., digital sticky notes on Miro) or recordings as many times as they need versus having to make an additional effort to record the session (via meeting notes, or storing artifacts).
- *Data manipulation:* Most digital artifacts allow easy creation, editing, duplication (e.g., copy and paste), and searching. For instance, instead of flipping through notes, one can use keywords and phrases to quickly locate key information.
- *Multimedia integration and hyperlinking:* Digital documents allow for embedding or linking to web resources for a multimodal experience, an experience that physical documents cannot match.
- *And much more:* With the use of AI becoming ubiquitous in technological tools, the opportunities for data manipulation continue to evolve. These opportunities could include improved workflows (catching up on information, creation of documents from scratch, brainstorming), and organizing and remixing information.

THE COSTS OF IMPLEMENTING INTERACTIVE SYNCHRONOUS HYFLEX

While the benefits of implementing Interactive Synchronous HyFlex may be compelling, the model also introduces layers of complexity that demand intentional preparation. Our goal is to equip you with a clear understanding of these challenges—from the viewpoints of both the teacher who is designing and delivering the course and the students who will be learning in this environment. We hope that seeing both perspectives helps you to decide whether this approach is viable for your classroom at this time.

TECHNOLOGICAL COMPLEXITY

TEACHER PERSPECTIVE

At first glance, adding simple technological additions such as Microsoft Teams, conference microphone/speaker pucks, and personal headphones into our workflow can seem like minor tweaks. To be clear, they are minor but, in our experience, instructors can feel pulled in multiple directions as they attempt to remain

FIGURE 1.6 Sometimes class can feel like the inside of a cockpit with all of the many things you need to do. SOURCE: Taiki Ishikawa (Unsplash)

visible to both their remote and face-to-face students during live teaching (figure 1.6 is a representation of the complexity instructors and students experience when trying something new). When you are juggling multiple software, facilitating discussions, and troubleshooting student problems, it's easy to feel that way. However, as you continue to gain experience, you learn where to click, to anticipate typical hiccups, and to facilitate both remote and face-to-face students. That said, occasional technical glitches—like a lost internet connection or a software update breaking your usual settings—are inevitable and require a willingness to adapt and stay calm under pressure.

STUDENT PERSPECTIVE

For students, the technological complexity can feel daunting at first, particularly for those who may not feel very tech-savvy. It is additional work for students to navigate simultaneous in-class and remote conversations within blended groups. On the plus side, there are many conveniences associated with the use of digital tools, such as having the flexibility to attend class from anywhere, access to screen recordings, chat-based interactions (e.g., useful for feedback sessions), and live transcripts.

COGNITIVE COMPLEXITY

TEACHER PERSPECTIVE

Interactive Synchronous HyFlex requires that instructors maintain engagement across two modalities simultaneously: face-to-face and remote. It is easy, and sometimes unavoidable, to pay more attention to whichever group is in front of you. While most students will understand the challenge of sharing instructor time among a large group of students, it means they may have to wait for your attention. One effective way to be responsive to all modalities is to recruit additional personnel—a teaching assistant or even a responsible student in the room with you—to monitor the chat and remote participants in real time. In our forty-student classroom, for example, an undergraduate TA keeps a special lookout for remote students' interactions (comments, questions, or support), ensuring no one is left out.

STUDENT PERSPECTIVE

From a student's viewpoint, cognitive complexity arises in managing the flow of class activities and group work across different modes. Remote students must figure out how to signal for help, ask questions, and collaborate with classmates who are physically together at a table. Face-to-face students, meanwhile, might try to juggle a face-to-face conversation while also keeping an eye on chat messages so their remote teammates aren't ignored. Some students thrive on having multiple ways to engage—such as speaking aloud, using text, or contributing to collaborative whiteboards—while others feel their mental energy is stretched thin by toggling between real-life discussion and virtual updates. While acknowledging this complexity, our students have often articulated that learning how to effectively navigate these channels is a key skill that will benefit them in future hybrid work settings.

PLANNING

TEACHER PERSPECTIVE

Designing an Interactive Synchronous HyFlex course requires careful upfront planning, from establishing clear expectations to configuring your learning management system (LMS) and collaboration tools so both face-to-face and remote students have equitable access. Adopting a digital-first approach—say, using an online whiteboard instead of a physical one—ensures that everyone can engage fully, though it can feel time-intensive at the outset. Chapter 2 offers specific strategies to streamline your planning so you can focus on teaching, not troubleshooting.

STUDENT PERSPECTIVE

Students notice (and appreciate) an instructor's advance planning. When the syllabus, daily schedules, and group project tools are all well organized in the LMS, students can access what they need in class, or from anywhere with the internet. At the same time, students do need to spend time thinking about what modality will work for them on any given day. Instructors can coach students into making decisions that will most benefit them.

DESIGN PRINCIPLES OF THE INTERACTIVE SYNCHRONOUS HYFLEX MODEL

The Interactive Synchronous HyFlex Model is built on the principle of being accessible to instructors and institutions to benefit students. It has three major features:

FIGURE 1.7 Students do not need specialized equipment to participate in a HyFlex classroom. Though additional equipment can be useful, their laptop and headphones are sufficient to get started on your HyFlex journey. SOURCE: Shawn Farrington

1. Low overhead: It is designed to be used with little specialized equipment (see figure 1.7—it's just a laptop and earbuds).
2. Student autonomy: Students are given the choice to attend class in the way that best suits them.
3. Accessibility: It supports the principles of UDL to produce a more accessible classroom.

1. LOW OVERHEAD: GETTING STARTED IS EASY

In a higher education setting, you likely already have access to most of the hardware and software you need to adapt a course. The most important technological requirements that constitute the Interactive Synchronous HyFlex model are as follows:

- *Readily available hardware:* The Interactive Synchronous Model makes use of the reality that students usually bring their own laptops, tablets, and/or phones with them to college. We leverage the microphones and cameras already built into these devices and avoid the setup required of additional equipment. However, we do offer a few loaner devices (older Chromebooks in a laptop cart) in case students need them in class.
- *High-speed internet:* College campuses typically offer high-speed internet in and out of classrooms, which is sufficient for collaborative and distributed work software.
- *Videoconferencing and instant messaging software:* Most higher education institutes provide access to videoconferencing and instant messaging software such as Microsoft Office 365 or Zoom. We use Microsoft Teams because it has specific features that match our needs, including a convenient single log-in associated with our students' authentication routines. For the purposes of our book, we acknowledge the ability of this type of software to do much more than simple videoconferencing by referring to it as collaboration software.
- *Distributed work software:* All of the software we use in the classroom is free for students to use or has a free to use education version. We use Google Docs, which is available for free for collaborating on documents, presentations, and spreadsheets. For online whiteboarding sessions, we use Miro and Figma, which offer free educational accounts for students and instructors. Finally, screen capturing software (e.g., native software such as Mac's

screenshot app, Snagit, Camtasia, and Screencast-O-Matic) are available through higher education institutes or are free use.

- *(Recommended) Conferencing microphone:* Proper audio is crucial to Interactive Synchronous HyFlex classrooms. While not strictly necessary, we recommend the use of conferencing microphones (such as handheld or desktop speaker/mic pucks) to capture the room's audio effectively. They ensure that remote students can clearly hear and participate in the classroom conversation, fostering a more inclusive environment. An additional benefit of using a conferencing microphone versus a laptop microphone is that the conferencing microphone can better avoid the distracting clicking sounds of typing.
- *(Recommended) Headphones:* When you or your students need to check in with remote or blended groups, headphones are helpful. They allow you to listen to the audio of the remote person clearly without disturbing those around you (e.g., over the classroom speakers).

EXAMPLE

Student Requirements Communicated in the Syllabus Related to the Interactive Synchronous HyFlex Model

Informed learning resources: No textbook. Standard office supplies for prototyping. Students will be informed of what supplies to procure for class activities on Purdue's Brightspace LMS. A limited number of Chromebooks will be available for use in class. Students will need a Gmail account for Chromebook and Google Drive use.

Software/web resources: Microsoft Teams app or web app.

Hardware requirements: Device with webcam to access Brightspace, Microsoft Teams, and Google Docs—laptop is preferred; fully charged batteries and power supply/battery charger; stable internet connection; headphones with microphone or earbuds with microphone preferred.

Brightspace learning management system: Access the course via Purdue's Brightspace LMS. Begin with the Start Here tab, which describes how the course Brightspace is organized. It is strongly suggested that you explore and become familiar not only with the site navigation but with content and resources available for this course. See the Student Services widget on the campus homepage for resources such as Technology Help, Academic Help, Campus Resources, and Protect Purdue.

QUICK TIP 	**What and How Specialized Equipment Can Help**
	You can choose to invest in more specialized equipment for your classroom. See chapter 4 (vignettes) for different setups.

2. STUDENT AUTONOMY: MORE ROBUST ATTENDANCE

Each day students can decide what mode of attendance is right for them. Sometimes, attending class face-to-face is impractical and having the flexibility to attend synchronously online can empower those who would have been unable to attend otherwise to participate.

> *As long as you have a computer and internet connection, you are able to be there and learn live. You can just choose whatever environment is the best for you. It's nice to be able to go wherever you want; you can still do it. But also, if you need help, and you want to go in person, you have that option as well. So, it's nice to have options. And it's also just kind of nice to have it available kind of wherever and have no pressure to be in person. If you have something going on, you can easily just kind of do that. So, it's really accessible. And it's really nice to have.*
> —STUDENT REFLECTION, FALL 2020

3. ACCESSIBILITY: MORE WAYS TO ENGAGE

The Interactive Synchronous HyFlex model includes several principles of inclusive learning environments that cater to diverse learning needs. This model is closely aligned with the UDL framework, which focuses on offering multiple ways for students to engage, perceive, and express their learning to meet a wide range of needs and abilities (CAST 2024). See the Further Reading box that follows to learn how HyFlex aligns with the three principles of UDL.

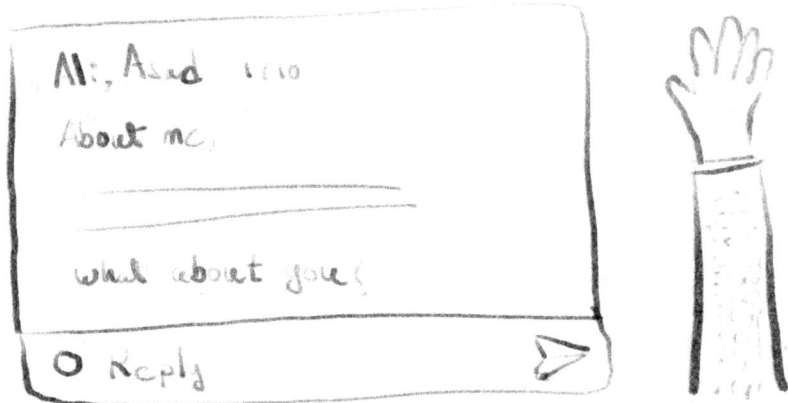

FIGURE 1.8 There are multiple ways to engage in HyFlex classrooms. For instance, students can reply in a chat or raise their hands in the classroom. SOURCE: Abdul Moeed Asad (Co-author)

FURTHER READING

HyFlex and UDL

Multiple Means of Engagement

Instruction in the Interactive Synchronous HyFlex model offers students flexibility in how they attend class (e.g., face-to-face or virtually) and participate in discussions (e.g., verbally or by typing in the Microsoft Teams chat), fostering individual choice and autonomy. Students also have access to digital course materials before, during, and after class through the LMS and class recordings, which can significantly enhance engagement with course content.

For instance, students who feel overwhelmed during live sessions can review recorded videos at their own pace, helping them persist without falling behind. Additionally, the Interactive Synchronous HyFlex model ensures consistent communication channels (e.g., email and chat), allowing students to access support and resources, even if they miss class or encounter difficulties with traditional participation methods.

FURTHER READING

HyFlex and UDL *(continued)*

Multiple Means of Representation
Features of Interactive Synchronous HyFlex instruction, such as live auto-transcription, make content accessible to d/Deaf or hard of hearing students, non-native English speakers, and students who may find it difficult to understand varying accents of spoken English. Additionally, closed captions in recorded videos can benefit students with attention challenges or those who prefer reading along to reinforce their understanding. Offering access to classroom recordings with features like playback control and captioning in English also ensures that all students can revisit key concepts of the lesson and understand the material at their own pace.

Multiple Means of Action and Expression
Providing options for participation, whether through verbal contributions or typing in chat (see figure 1.8), not only optimizes student engagement but also allows them to express themselves in ways that suit their preferences.

Instructors further enhance accessibility by using a variety of digital tools that facilitate collaboration between both face-to-face and remote students. By leveraging technology, the HyFlex model ensures that all students, regardless of location, can interact, collaborate, share ideas, and demonstrate their knowledge, thus promoting equal participation.

Additionally, Interactive Synchronous HyFlex instruction allows students to submit assignments digitally, either in real time or asynchronously. Students can draw or write some of their assignments on paper and submit it as a picture, or they can draw online and submit the digital version of their assignment.

RELATED SECTION

Videoconferencing Software Offers Multiple Affordances

See the section "The Use of Technology Enables New Capabilities" earlier in this chapter for how specific digital affordances make interactive synchronous classrooms more accessible.

COMMUNITY OF INQUIRY (COI)

Cultivating a strong sense of community is essential in a HyFlex format. Instructors must make an effort to connect with both in-person and virtual students to foster a positive and inclusive learning environment.
—DR. NEELAKSHI MAJUMDAR, INSTRUCTOR 2016–2022

We grounded the design and facilitation of the Interactive Synchronous HyFlex model in the Community of Inquiry (CoI) framework. The CoI framework offers a method for designing effective collaborative learning experiences through the consideration and creation of three components: social presence, cognitive presence, and teaching presence. Although the CoI framework was originally created to guide the development of meaningful online learning environments, it has been used in blended contexts to inform the creation of effective online elements. When using the CoI framework to inform the development and facilitation of blended learning environments, careful consideration must be given to how specific design elements aid learners and are combined to support learning across modalities. Detailed information regarding the CoI framework can be found at the Community of Inquiry website (https://www.thecommunityofinquiry.org/coi).

SOCIAL PRESENCE

Social presence is the extent to which students are able to project themselves socially and emotionally as real people in online learning environments, fostering a sense of belonging. Social presence consists of three components: open communication (together with the instructor, learners feel a sense of dedication to a team), group cohesion (the instructor and learners interact as they complete meaningful cognitive collaborative activities), and affective (the instructor and learners share feelings, beliefs, and values). As students and instructors interact and collaboratively navigate a learning process, social presence is created in various ways, such as sharing pictures or video to project face and voice, using greetings and names when interacting with others, and acknowledging others' ideas.

COGNITIVE PRESENCE

Cognitive presence is the extent to which learners are actively engaged in the learning process, developing skills like critical thinking, problem-solving, and knowledge construction. Cognitive presence involves three elements: triggering events (learners consider a problem or question), exploration (learners analyze the problem through researching and interacting with diverse perspectives), and integration/resolution (learners develop a solution or resolution for the problem at hand). Cognitive presence may be enacted through various instructional approaches: case-based learning, debate, reflection, hands-on projects, and so on.

TEACHING PRESENCE

Teaching presence includes the methods and strategies that instructors use as they design, facilitate, and guide meaningful learning experiences. Teaching presence consists of three components: design and organization (structuring and organizing a course to support learning and interaction), facilitating discourse (prompting the consideration of problems through open conversation, analysis, and reflection), and direct instruction (guiding learners toward meaningful learning outcomes). Teaching presence is created in many ways, including clarifying content; offering reminders and examples; sharing alternative viewpoints, summaries, and tips; and providing feedback and demonstrations.

RESEARCH SPOTLIGHT

How Does Interactive Synchronous HyFlex Affect Students' Sense of Presence?

See chapter 5 for details.

Refer to Study 1 to explore how the Interactive Synchronous HyFlex model influences students' perceptions of social, teaching, and cognitive presence.

FINAL WORDS ON CONSIDERING INTERACTIVE SYNCHRONOUS HYFLEX

With this chapter we hope we have provided you with enough reasons to consider both why you might want to implement Interactive Synchronous HyFlex and the issues that may arise during implementation. Interactive Synchronous HyFlex can better meet the needs of your students than a traditional classroom, allowing them to participate in more enabling and accessible ways.

The benefits of Interactive Synchronous HyFlex can be difficult to visualize until they are reflected in your day-to-day life: Reduced disruptions can mean getting more done (e.g., despite weather events) and less instructional effort to bring absent students back up to speed because of more robust participation in the classroom. And importantly, students with physical and learning disabilities have multiple tools to support their specific needs.

The model has low overhead, and you likely already have access to most of the technologies to get started. However, transitioning to the model requires careful planning and execution. If you're curious to try Interactive Synchronous HyFlex, the subsequent chapters offer practical guidance on how you might go about implementing it in your context.

REFERENCES

Beatty, Brian, ed. 2019. *Hybrid-Flexible Course Design: Implementing Student-Directed Hybrid Classes*. EdTech Books.

CAST. 2024. "Universal Design for Learning Guidelines Version 3.0." https://udlguidelines.cast.org.

Hietala, Janne. 2019. "Why Do We Spend All That Time Searching for Information at Work?" *Valamis* (blog). https://www.valamis.com/blog/why-do-we-spend-all-that-time-searching-for-information-at-work.

2

TRANSITIONING TO AN INTERACTIVE SYNCHRONOUS HYFLEX CLASSROOM

Chapter 1 introduced the potential of Interactive Synchronous HyFlex classrooms, while the focus of chapter 2 is on how to put it into practice. This chapter offers a practical roadmap for implementing HyFlex as it addresses common questions and concerns. We envision this chapter to be read before the start of the term when instructors have the headspace to plan out their courses. However, we imagine that instructors will need to fine-tune their approach throughout the semester. Revisiting the chapter whenever you feel the need may be helpful.

This chapter has three parts: setting expectations, setting up the classroom environment, and preparing classroom activities. Setting expectations will help instructors manage key challenges with adopting Interactive Synchronous HyFlex, such as whether students choose to attend remotely and disengage. Learning to effectively set up the classroom environment will help to create a conducive environment for effective instruction (as shown in figure 2.1). Finally, preparing classroom activities aligned with key Interactive Synchronous HyFlex affordances will help to maximize the learning experience for all students.

FIGURE 2.1 A transition can seem daunting but students in higher education are able to take ownership of their own learning after an initial introduction. SOURCE: Shawn Farrington

PART 1: SETTING EXPECTATIONS

HOW FLEXIBLE SHOULD YOUR HYFLEX COURSE BE?

Interactive Synchronous HyFlex offers numerous benefits (see "Why Consider Implementing HyFlex Classrooms" in chapter 1), but ultimately what works best is what is appropriate for both your and your students' needs (see figure 2.2). To understand your preferences, consider the questions that follow. We will consider students' needs in the section "Who Gets to Be Remote (and for How Long)?" later in this chapter.

FIGURE 2.2 You can tailor your course to be as flexible as best suits your and your student's needs. SOURCE: Abdul Moeed Asad (Co-author)

QUESTION	DESCRIPTION	EXAMPLE EXPECTATIONS*
Do you have a preference for face-to-face or remote attendance? Why?	Instructors may prefer face-to-face attendance over remote attendance. If you do have a preference, communicate it with your students, including reasons for this preference. However, be sure you are not creating a culture of exclusion. Ensure that students who attend remotely are treated with respect and their contributions valued.	*Attending class face-to-face is a superior experience because [add your rationale here]. Please prioritize coming to the classroom. That said, we understand that life happens, and we appreciate the work you do regardless of your mode of attendance.*
Do your expectations for attendance vary by class session?	Depending on your needs, certain class meetings can be fully remote (e.g., if the instructor will be traveling) or fully face-to-face (e.g., classes that require work with equipment). You can set clear expectations in advance for these sessions.	*I will be traveling in the fifth week of the semester. In that week, we will have class remotely. If you prefer to meet with your group in this room, the classroom will be open for you. You will have [resources like TAs being available to the class].*
Who decides when students should be face-to-face or remote?	Some instructors may decide to have students ask for permission to be remote and/or only allow it in special circumstances. Other instructors might not have any restrictions on the mode of student attendance but may want to be notified so they can facilitate participation.	*Example 1: You do not need to ask permission to attend class remotely. If you suspect you have a contagious illness, you should only attend class remotely.* *Example 2: Please let your teammates and me know if you will be remote. We want to make sure we're able to help you have a meaningful experience.*

*Ways instructors might communicate with their students.

> **RELATED SECTION**
>
> **How Can You Best Respond to the Needs of Your Students?**
>
> Students have many diverse needs (e.g., caregiving, part-time work, health issues), and even if they wish to let us know in advance, they may not be able to (e.g., timing of needs, fear of judgment, time constraints).
>
> Offering a degree of flexibility can encourage students to make decisions based on what is best for them (versus other pressures such as trying to appease the instructor, for example).
>
> Read more in "Who Gets to Be Remote (and for How Long)?" later in this chapter.

In our design classroom, we strongly encourage face-to-face attendance when working with physical prototypes so that students can take advantage of their group's pooled resources (time and material). Other times, our encouragement varies. We, as instructors, generally prefer face-to-face attendance, but we respect students' need to attend class remotely and let them make the determination. While we believe students usually make thoughtful decisions, we recognize their decisions may not always be in their own best interest (see Kirschner and van Merriënboer 2013). Read the next section to see how we prevent students from misusing the flexibility granted to them.

ANTICIPATING CHALLENGES

From our work, we find that instructors are concerned about the quality of engagement of students participating remotely. Our teaching experience and research findings offer a few key insights.

First, you will not be teaching to an empty classroom. If you communicate that face-to-face participation is expected and remote participation is available as needed, students will cooperate, especially when you provide a rationale.

Second, we have noticed that some remote students will not engage. We see their name (they are logged on) but there is no response and no contribution from them. While this occurs, we have also seen this happen in the physical classroom as well. Students can fall asleep or get distracted. The key is active, meaningful engagement. Engaging all learners actively minimizes the issue for remote and face-to-face students. If you forget about the remote students, they may forget about you.

Our research indicates that HyFlex classrooms perform as well as or better than face-to-face-only instruction (see chapter 5, Study 5). Still, students who attend remotely sometimes struggle more than their face-to-face peers. However, this doesn't mean remote learning causes disengagement. Our research suggests that the autonomy and flexibility afforded through the Interactive Synchronous HyFlex model benefit most students, but some students may need extra scaffolding to navigate the course remotely.

Additionally, some learners with a tendency toward disengagement may gravitate to remote participation. In other words, being remote may not be the cause of disengagement. For example, if a student is only moderately committed to the course, being remote may be tempting because it makes it easier to check out. Also, physical distance can make active contribution feel out of reach. Coaching students to make better participation choices can yield significant results.

To ensure a positive HyFlex experience, in this section we offer guidelines for explicitly stating expectations from the outset. This sets clear classroom norms and helps avoid potential misuse of the flexibility HyFlex offers.

WHO GETS TO BE REMOTE (AND FOR HOW LONG)?

One common instructor concern is how providing flexibility will influence classroom culture. From our experience, encouraging student autonomy by letting students decide how best to show up for class is important. If you have this concern and are worried about students taking too many remote days, you can clearly outline your expectations regarding who can attend remotely and for how long.

Here are some factors to consider when creating your expectations:

- *Equity: What are your students' needs, and how can they best perform in your class?* The option for remote attendance for students facilitates students that have health concerns or those with other obligations, like travel or family care. By allowing students to choose the mode that works for them on a daily basis, you support a more inclusive and accessible learning environment.
- *Autonomy: Can students choose to participate in class without facing cumbersome procedures?* Flexibility allows students to choose the preferred mode of engagement. This is especially important for nontraditional students and those with disabilities, who may have different needs.

> **QUICK TIP**
>
> **What if Students Are Unable to Join on Mandatory Face-to-Face or Remote Days?**
>
> If students are unable to join in the preferred mode, consider providing alternative ways to engage, such as recordings, discussion forums, and/or comparable assignments. This flexibility ensures that students who cannot attend in the recommended format still have meaningful opportunities to achieve the learning objectives.

- *Course goals: How does HyFlex align with your course objectives and central learning activities?* Most activities can be adapted for HyFlex, but if certain learning experiences work best or are only feasible in either a face-to-face or remote format, communicate these expectations early.
- *Classroom culture: How does the mode of attendance affect your classroom culture?* The mode of attendance may affect classroom culture. Some of our instructors feel that attending class face-to-face has social and productivity benefits, which positively contribute to classroom culture. While they ensure that the process of attending class remotely is easy, they impose additional conditions that prevent remote attendance from becoming habitual (see the next section for suggestions on what to do).

REMOTE STUDENTS: ARE THEY ENGAGED?

You may wonder about the degree to which remote students engage with course content. For face-to-face students, instructors are cautiously optimistic when students are making eye contact and paying attention. While our research suggests that remote attendance does not inherently lead to worse outcomes, active participation and accountability remain crucial in any mode of participation and are slightly more challenging for remote students (see figure 2.3).

To get a better sense of remote student engagement, clearly communicate and enforce your participation requirements, expecting verbal, chat, or other forms of interaction. If you have reason to believe your students are skirting accountability, you can limit the number of times students can consecutively attend class remotely or more carefully monitor student participation. Additionally, you can require or strongly encourage the use of webcams to increase student visibility.

FIGURE 2.3 For brief moments, it can seem as if we're speaking into a void, but our fears may be overblown. SOURCE: Abdul Moeed Asad (Co-author)

RESEARCH SPOTLIGHT

How Does Interactive Synchronous HyFlex Affect Academic Performance for Face-to-Face and Remote Students?

See chapter 5 for details.

Refer to Study 5 for our findings on the impact of the Interactive Synchronous HyFlex model on student academic performance.

ARE REMOTE STUDENTS GETTING THE SUPPORT THEY NEED?

Sometimes remote students would like to engage but don't know how, or they might be ignored.

REMOTE STUDENTS MAY NOT KNOW HOW TO ENGAGE	FACE-TO-FACE INSTRUCTORS AND/OR STUDENTS MAY BE IGNORING REMOTE STUDENTS
Unclear expectations: Students might be unsure of when to speak, how to signal that they have a question, or what level of participation is expected. *Tech illiteracy and issues:* Students are sometimes unable to navigate interfaces or experience technical glitches that disrupt their ability to hear, see, or be heard clearly.	*Lack of visibility:* Without a physical presence, remote students can be unintentionally forgotten or ignored. *Naive hybrid etiquette:* Face-to-face students might not be aware of best practices to ensure that their remote peers can follow along smoothly. Remote participants might feel isolated if face-to-face group members don't actively include them.

REMOTE STUDENTS MAY NOT KNOW HOW TO ENGAGE	FACE-TO-FACE INSTRUCTORS AND/OR STUDENTS MAY BE IGNORING REMOTE STUDENTS
	Attitudinal issues: There can be a lack of value placed on the contributions of remote students (some face-to-face students feel that they made the effort to get to the classroom and their peers did not), leading to their exclusion from meaningful participation. Over time, remote students may participate less and less if their ideas are consistently dismissed, creating a downward spiral of disengagement.

To bridge this gap, the following intentional strategies are essential:

- *Establish clear ground rules:* Periodically, the instructor or the group should outline clear expectations for participation from all attendees, whether they are remote or face-to-face. Explain how to ask questions, share ideas, and signal technical difficulties.
- *Perform periodic check-ins:* The instructor or the group should regularly ask remote participants and their face-to-face teammates directly if they have questions, need clarification, or are experiencing any issues. This shows you value their input and are attentive to their needs.
- *Foster peer support:* Encourage face-to-face group members to actively engage their remote peers. This could involve asking direct questions, summarizing key points, or simply checking in to see how they are doing.

QUICK TIP

Early Communication, Although Optional, Can Be Helpful

Having students communicate in advance if they are going to be remote can help you and student groups facilitate remote students' inclusion into the classroom. The remote student's group can help them get the support they need and you as their instructor can be mindful to check in on their group for support.

- *Use inclusive technology:* Utilize collaborative tools like shared digital whiteboards, polls, or breakout rooms that allow remote participants to contribute in a variety of ways. If using a physical whiteboard in the room, consider pointing a laptop camera directly at the whiteboard to facilitate easy viewing for remote peers. Share with students how to enlarge the view from the camera that is showing the whiteboard to make their view larger and clearer.

ARE FACE-TO-FACE STUDENTS GETTING THE SUPPORT THEY NEED?
On the flip side, face-to-face students may not know how to support their remote counterparts or may feel overwhelmed with managing the process.

Instructors can build student capacity to effectively facilitate remote peers by modeling inclusive practices and practicing technology as a class as follows:

- To model behavior, narrate how you go about setting up the classroom for HyFlex participation across modalities (e.g., *I will get out the conference speaker so that everyone is able to hear us. I'll connect it with the Bluetooth on my computer and then ensure that the settings are all correct.*).
- As practice, give students simple assignments that help them get comfortable using key features such as creating posts (e.g., asking students to introduce themselves using the chat tool) and sharing files (e.g., asking students to share a file using collaboration software). Another simple way to build capacity is by asking students to explicitly practice skills (e.g., *Say "Hi" in the Teams chat if you're in class today.*).

EXAMPLE EXPECTATIONS
Here are some examples of classroom expectations.

EXAMPLE

HyFlex Attendance Guideline Example 1

We want you to get the most out of this class, including experiencing the energy and dynamic interaction of face-to-face learning. While you're welcome to engage remotely whenever it best suits your needs, please prioritize coming to class face-to-face as often as possible.

EXAMPLE

HyFlex Attendance Guideline Example 1 (*continued*)

Here's how remote attendance works:

No permission needed (up to two consecutive sessions): You can choose to attend remotely for up to two class sessions in a row without asking permission beforehand. We recommend that you let us know in advance if you plan to be remote so that we can help you participate in class, but it is not required.

Permission needed (more than two consecutive sessions): If you need to attend remotely for more than two sessions in a row, please talk to your instructor ahead of time. We'll work with you to find a solution that supports your learning and accommodates your circumstances.

We're committed to creating an inclusive and accessible learning environment, so don't hesitate to reach out if you have any questions or concerns.

EXAMPLE

HyFlex Attendance Guideline Example 2

We will use Microsoft Teams to complement participation in our face-to-face course.
- Microsoft Teams join code: [*code*]
- Join the Microsoft Teams meeting [*link to recurring Microsoft Teams meeting*]
    - for remote synchronous participation (only when face-to-face participation is impractical)
    - when you're in the classroom to share screens (mute audio)
- Review meeting recordings [*link to Microsoft Teams meeting recordings folder*] in the "Files" tab of the general channel. The meetings should automatically record. Alert us if not!
- Use the chat feature to message/video call your peers.
- Use "@team" in the general channel [*link to Microsoft Teams general channel*] to alert everyone.
- Watch six-minute video on navigating Microsoft Teams. (https://www.youtube.com/watch?v=q_nS17-4uBY).

RESEARCH SPOTLIGHT 	**Does Self-Regulation Influence Participation Choices in HyFlex?** *See chapter 5 for details.* Refer to Study 7 to investigate the relationship between students' self-regulation skills and their participation choices in a HyFlex class.

RESEARCH SPOTLIGHT 	**Does HyFlex Fulfill Students' Psychological Needs?** *See chapter 5 for details.* Refer to Study 3 to quantitatively examine the extent to which the HyFlex model met students' basic psychological needs compared to a traditional face-to-face-only environment.

DEVELOPING EXPECTATIONS FOR MEANINGFUL INTERACTIONS

We used the Community of Inquiry (CoI) framework as a guide when developing expectations for student interactions and facilitating our research. The CoI framework may help you anticipate challenges in delivering a HyFlex course.

As you design a HyFlex course, grounding your work in established educational frameworks will help you to identify indicators of success and provide focus for improvements. Because the addition of a remote option was a new element for us and many of our students, we used the CoI framework (see figure 2.4) to help guide the inclusion of the remote modality of the HyFlex classroom. As we think of classrooms as learning communities, the framework helps create spaces of meaningful interaction, deep thinking, and effective teaching. The table that follows provides example expectations to share with students for how to engage in the classroom.

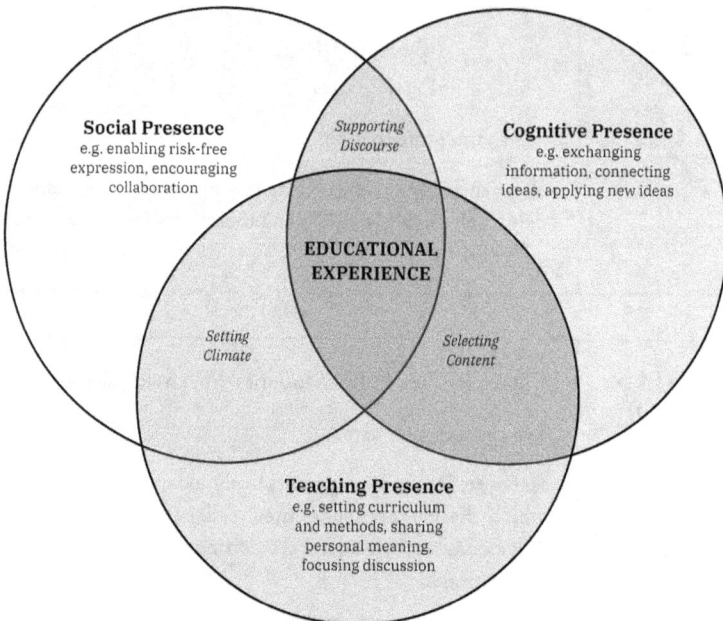

FIGURE 2.4 The Community of Inquiry framework. SOURCE: Adapted from Garrison and Vaughan (2018). In the Creative Commons.

COI ELEMENT	QUESTIONS TO CONSIDER WHEN SETTING EXPECTATIONS	EXAMPLES IN PRACTICE*
Social Presence		
The extent to which students are able to project themselves socially and emotionally in a remote learning environment, fostering a sense of belonging. Social presence includes three areas: open communication, group cohesion, and affective considerations.	What is expected use for web cameras (e.g., all students using, only remote students using, optional during whole group discussions or during small group breakouts)? How are students expected to indicate their intended or current attendance modality?	Our Microsoft Teams channels are for your use. You can ask questions in the #general channel, and use the #random channel for memes or personal updates (e.g., club announcements). At the beginning of each class, please indicate in the Teams chat whether you're remote.

COI ELEMENT	QUESTIONS TO CONSIDER WHEN SETTING EXPECTATIONS	EXAMPLES IN PRACTICE*
Social Presence (continued)		
	How will remote students be acknowledged by both the instructor and teammates? What strategies and resources are necessary to accommodate students in teamwork? What methods can simultaneously involve both face-to-face and remote students?	Turning your camera on when you're remote is probably the easiest and best way for you to make this work. If you can see the person when they're remote, they can see you. It should work both ways. At the beginning of each class, you should log into Teams, whether you're face-to-face or remote.
Cognitive Presence		
The extent to which learners are actively engaged in the learning process, developing skills like critical thinking, problem-solving, and knowledge construction. Cognitive presence involves using triggering events, exploration, integration, and resolution to facilitate learners to consider ideas, collaborate, and apply understanding.	How will students receive directions and guidance on how to complete course activities that accommodate both face-to-face and remote students? How are students expected to communicate and interact with peers and the instructor across modalities? What tools and considerations are necessary to support student work in blended and remote groups? How will groups be set up to complete course work (e.g., mixed modalities, remote students grouped)?	Once a group is done presenting, help your peers improve their designs by asking thoughtful questions in the Feedback thread on Teams. If you were the group presenting, respond to your peers' feedback. You can respond to other people by using the @ sign and begin writing their name. Once you start typing you should be able to select their name from the dropdown menu. Please use the remote whiteboard to brainstorm ideas related to Project 3 topics.

COI ELEMENT	QUESTIONS TO CONSIDER WHEN SETTING EXPECTATIONS	EXAMPLES IN PRACTICE*
Cognitive Presence (*continued*)		
	How are all students expected to demonstrate engagement while collaborating and applying understanding?	For my three students working remotely, please work together to complete in-class activities by discussing and collaborating through Teams.
Teaching Presence		
The instructor's role in creating the learning environment includes setting the curriculum, facilitating class, and providing feedback. Teaching presence includes three areas: design and organization, facilitating discourse, and direct instruction.	How will content be displayed and shared so that all students, regardless of modality, can easily follow class activities? How will students be directed to participate in class activities and work with remote teammates? What strategies can be used to make both face-to-face and remote students feel welcome? How can the instructor provide feedback to all students in effective and meaningful ways? How can the instructor offer support and clarification to students across modalities?	Instructors can make themselves available and offer support to students in multiple ways in HyFlex classrooms. If you have a group member who's working remotely, then your team needs to be on Microsoft Teams. You will have a private channel on Teams for your team to use for communication that the rest of the class will not have access to. During each class, I share my screen and turn on my video, and I have my TA help with monitoring the chat if there are questions.

*Things instructors might communicate to their students. (These examples are from Microsoft Teams, but other tools can be used in similar ways.)

RESEARCH SPOTLIGHT 	**How Is Instructor Presence Established in HyFlex Classrooms?** See chapter 5 for details. Refer to Study 10 to investigate how instructor presence is established in HyFlex classrooms and whether variations in instructor approaches are associated with student perceptions of instructor presence.
RESEARCH SPOTLIGHT 	**How Do First-Year Design Students View Interactive Synchronous HyFlex Through the Lens of the Community of Inquiry Framework?** See chapter 5 for details. Refer to Study 1 to explore how the Interactive Synchronous HyFlex model influences students' perceptions of social, teaching, and cognitive presence.

PART 2: SETTING UP THE CLASSROOM ENVIRONMENT FOR INTERACTIVE SYNCHRONOUS HYFLEX

Before the start of the semester, we configure and make adjustments to our learning management system (LMS) and collaboration software to anticipate the needs of both our face-to-face students and remote learners (as represented by figure 2.5). The advantages of setting up the LMS and collaboration software for Interactive Synchronous HyFlex not only make the classroom more accessible for remote learners but add a layer of robustness for face-to-face students (e.g., snow days are no longer a reason to skip school—unfortunate news for some of us). Creating a classroom in this way aligns with universal design for learning (UDL) principles to promote accessibility and inclusivity for all students.

On a day when a technology challenge occurs (e.g., the HDMI connection is not working—a common enough occurrence in our classroom), rather than losing valuable time, preloaded resources in the LMS (e.g., presentation slides and

FIGURE 2.5 Setting up an Interactive Synchronous HyFlex learning experience is not drastically different from preparing for a traditional classroom! We make two major recommendations— posting everything on an LMS and using collaboration software like Microsoft Teams. SOURCE: Abdul Moeed Asad (Co-author)

streaming links) allow remote students to stay engaged through the LMS and face-to-face students to quickly join remotely and view an instructor's shared screen if needed. This setup minimizes disruptions, supports multiple access points, and promotes seamless transitions during what might otherwise be a large technical glitch.

RELATED SECTION	How Is Interactive Synchronous HyFlex Related to UDL?
	See "Design Principles of the Interactive Synchronous HyFlex Model" in chapter 1 to read more about the ways Interactive Synchronous HyFlex aligns with UDL.

HOW TO CONFIGURE YOUR LMS TO SUPPORT INTERACTIVE SYNCHRONOUS HYFLEX ENVIRONMENTS

We recommend setting up a class LMS so that **all** students have **easy** access to **important resources**. Let us break down what we mean.

INCLUSIVE OF ALL (REMOTE AND FACE-TO-FACE) STUDENTS
An LMS can help ensure that each student has equal access to classroom resources. For example, if a student club wants to distribute flyers, you can upload

digital versions to the LMS, ensuring that both face-to-face and remote students have the same information. This UDL approach removes barriers to learning by making resources available in multiple formats and locations, which is especially valuable for students who miss class or have varying needs for accessing information.

EASY TO ACCESS

An LMS that is effectively organized is easy to access. Organize yours in a way that works best for your instructional approach. Some instructors structure their LMS using one or a combination of the following ways:

- Modules-based (Project 1, Project 2, and so on)
- Affinity-based (Resources, Assignments, and so on)
- Time-period-based (session-based or week-based)

We organize our LMS (currently Brightspace) using a session-based approach, and we share all content at the beginning of the semester. This structure benefits all students by setting clear expectations for where materials will appear each week, which can reduce cognitive load and facilitate a sense of autonomy—both of which are key to UDL.

We recommend that before class you post in the LMS the resources that will be used in the classroom (e.g., presentation slides). If a student is absent, they will have access to everything they need to stay on track. This approach not only fosters inclusivity but also builds independence as students can access resources when they're most effective for their individual learning process.

IMPORTANT RESOURCES

Beyond assignment instructions and readings, our LMS contains important documents including the syllabus with our HyFlex participation expectations, how to communicate with the teaching staff, and how to sign up and use the classroom collaboration software (see figure 2.6).

While including these resources in the LMS is important, we also review them in class. Students may not necessarily take advantage of resources available to them just because they are available. Without explicit attention to a resource, students may not recognize its functionality and how it might help them to achieve their learning goals (Elen 2020).

Having these resources can make troubleshooting issues easier and result in significant time savings in a busy, large classroom. For example, an instructor can say to their students: *If you're having trouble accessing Microsoft Teams, you will find important information in the resources section located in Brightspace* (as depicted in figure 2.7). *If you need more assistance, please reach out and I'll be happy to figure things out with you.*

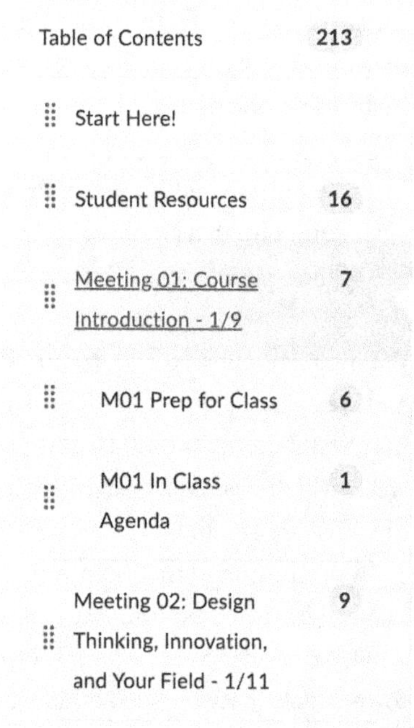

FIGURE 2.6 We use a time period-based setup in Brightspace so students know what they need to do before and during each session. SOURCE: Abdul Moeed Asad (Co-author)

Table of Contents	213
Start Here!	
Student Resources	16
Meeting 01: Course Introduction - 1/9	7
M01 Prep for Class	6
M01 In Class Agenda	1
Meeting 02: Design Thinking, Innovation, and Your Field - 1/11	9

FIGURE 2.7 In a forest, if a resource exists but you don't talk about it, does it really exist? How to set up and use your Collaboration Software. SOURCE: Abdul Moeed Asad (Co-author)

HOW TO SET UP AND USE YOUR COLLABORATION SOFTWARE

Collaboration software becomes the virtual extension of the classroom. A major benefit of using collaboration software is that all activity is easily accessible to both remote and face-to-face students (see figure 2.8). We currently use Microsoft Teams as our collaboration software, but other communication tools have similar features, including videoconferencing, threaded conversations, file sharing, and channels (or groups). Our approach to HyFlex using Microsoft Teams is likely generalizable to other software platforms such as Zoom, Google Meet, or others (although we haven't tested them).

At the beginning of the semester, we focus on using the Microsoft Teams general channel. We use this channel to make announcements, host classroom meetings, and store class recordings. We create additional team channels to facilitate small group meetings and design critiques (where we split the class in half).

As the course progresses, instructors create special purpose, session-specific, and small group channels as needed.

MS TEAMS: Review these instructions carefully even if you have used TEAMS before as they outline key steps and strategies to be successful in our course specifically. Download and install (preferred) MS TEAMS or use the web interface from Office.com. During class time you are required to have your webcam on so we can see each other. Keep your microphone muted until you are ready to contribute to minimize distractions. Note that attendance will be taken using MS TEAMS - so - you must log in and be interactive during each class meeting. If you have difficulty connecting, please let me know and we will discuss accommodations. Installing the MS TEAMS application provides you with closed captioning, video recording, screen sharing, and remote desktop control capabilities (the web version and mobile versions have limited features).

Critical - Before your first class meeting: Watch this 6 Minute MS TEAMS Student Use Video demonstrating how we will use TEAMS:

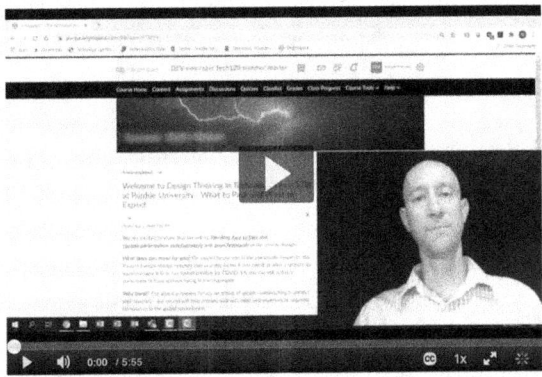

FIGURE 2.8 Part of what the resources section looks like in our course Brightspace.
SOURCE: Screenshot of Brightspace (Abdul Moeed Asad)

SPECIAL PURPOSE CHANNELS

Special purpose channels provide spaces for student communication. Here are three examples of special purpose channels:

- *Questions:* A dedicated space to encourage students to ask general questions related to the course (e.g., asking about due dates, clarifying assignment requirements).
- *Resources:* Where the instructor can post commonly referenced resources such as the syllabus and project rubrics.
- *Random:* Students can use this channel for personal updates, memes, club announcements, or other posts that do not neatly fit into other channels. A random channel can be an important space for students to discuss matters beyond the course and connect with each other.

In short, channels can be created to support individual course needs.

SESSION-SPECIFIC CHANNELS

Session-specific channels are time-bound. By managing activities through session-specific channels, keeping conversations organized is easy, as opposed to having large conversation threads in a single channel. Here are two examples of session-specific channels:

- *Introductions:* Students can connect with and get to know peers by sharing their hometowns, hobbies, majors, or other personal information while becoming familiar with Teams.
- *Project gallery:* Students post their projects, give presentations in class, and receive feedback in the channel by replying in the chat.

SMALL GROUP CHANNELS

Small group channels create spaces for collaboration. For example, for each group project, we create channels named after the project number and the group number (e.g., Project 02 Group 01; see figures 2.9 and 2.10), so that group 01 knows where they can host meetings, share files, and complete their work. Additionally, in the physical classroom, we typically label each table with numbers so each group knows where to meet (e.g., group 1 meets at table 1). This helps students know where to meet whether they are attending physically or virtually.

TRANSITIONING TO AN INTERACTIVE SYNCHRONOUS HYFLEX CLASSROOM / 41

FIGURE 2.9 The magic of our classroom happens in small groups, which collaborate regardless of individual mode of attendance. SOURCE: Abdul Moeed Asad (Co-author)

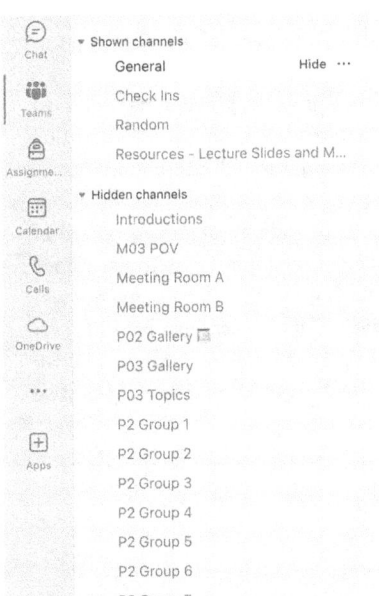

FIGURE 2.10 How one of our instructor's Microsoft Teams looks at the middle of the semester. Channels not frequently used or otherwise redundant can be hidden. SOURCE: Screenshot of Microsoft Teams (Abdul Moeed Asad)

THE FINE PRINT

Why Set Up Collaboration Software for Students' After Hours Use?

A significant amount of work in our course happens outside of class and as a group. To facilitate this work, we set up our classroom collaboration software, Microsoft Teams, as a central location to facilitate the experience. This approach has three key benefits: ease of use, preserving student privacy, and supporting accountability.

Ease of use: When students have useful established default virtual spaces (e.g., channels on Microsoft Teams where they can videoconference, chat, and share files), they are able to work on projects without having to focus on the logistical challenges of setting up communication channels in a fast-paced course (e.g., how to set up a personal group chat when a group member left class early).

Privacy: A significant concern in any collaborative environment is maintaining the privacy of participants. By using Microsoft Teams, students are not required to share personal contact information with their peers. Instead, they can engage through their student organizational identities. This separation helps protect their personal space and boundaries, reducing barriers for them to participate fully without the worry of overstepping privacy concerns.

Accountability: With group projects, group dynamics must be managed. Interactions using digital collaboration tools leave traces. These recorded interactions facilitate productive group dynamics. Recorded meetings and message histories provide an objective record of contributions and communications. This transparency not only helps in resolving conflicts but also encourages student accountability. Digital traces can be useful for instructors when they must mediate conflicts and for students when they need to reflect on their collaborative processes.

PART 3: PREPARING CLASSROOM ACTIVITIES FOR HYFLEX

In this section we offer questions for consideration to guide the design of Interactive Synchronous HyFlex classrooms. The model is a great default way to teach even on days when we do not have remote students. We believe our classroom still benefits from recordings, screen sharing, chat, and Teams channels to support any direct instruction from an instructor and team activities (as shown in Figure 2.11).

INSTRUCTIONAL APPROACH

- *How should I change my classroom activities for Interactive Synchronous HyFlex?* The main adjustment is ensuring that classroom activities are inclusive to both modalities. Most activities completed face-to-face can be done in blended groups. For instance, a typical brainstorming solution activity might include sticking Post-It notes to a whiteboard or blank wall so ideas are visual and can be organized.

FIGURE 2.11 We encourage the use of digital tools as classroom defaults to ensure our students are prepared to collaborate meaningfully in a blended context. SOURCE: Abdul Moeed Asad (Co-author)

Groups in Interactive Synchronous HyFlex can utilize a virtual whiteboard, like FigJam or Miro, to the same effect. While digital whiteboards have an initial learning curve, they offer a host of benefits that make classwork easier. We particularly appreciate their ability to work on templates and quickly share work as high-quality images.

RELATED SECTION

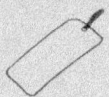

How to Work Digital-First Efficiently

Making available web links to relevant tools prepared ahead of time minimizes transition time in class should you have blended groups. If you don't already, consider utilizing Google or Microsoft cloud-based collaboration tools. If your institution uses a learning management software, consider adding all of your course material to it so it can be accessed from anywhere.

See the sections "Setting Up the Classroom Environment for Interactive Synchronous HyFlex" and "How to Set Up and Use Your Collaboration Software" for more tips on how to set up class to minimize transition time.

THE FINE PRINT

How Should You Structure Your Course?

We use a flipped and blended approach to structure our course because we believe these elements best support our HyFlex teaching practice. While a flipped and blended course structure can be a powerful way to help students learn in a HyFlex setting, it is by no means the only approach. Consider your own goals, resources, and teaching style to develop the format that best fits your context.

Flipped: In a flipped structure, instead of listening to lectures or other materials in class and then doing homework and group projects after class, students first engage with new content outside of class through videos, readings, or other resources. Then, they come to class prepared to discuss the material, work on problems, or engage in hands-on activities. In Interactive Synchronous HyFlex classrooms, a flipped structure allows all of your instructional material to be available online for all to view when they need it.

> **THE FINE PRINT**
>
>
>
> **How Should You Structure Your Course?** (*continued*)
>
> *Blended:* We synchronously blend (face-to-face and remote) student groups in the classroom. We create clear transitions from large group to small group work because of the overhead (transitioning usually takes two to five minutes) involved with making transitions. Instructors will cue their students to let them know of an incoming transition and what they need to do to be prepared. This includes where they need to go to start their meetings. In our classroom, we use channels to organize student meeting spaces (figure 2.10 shows what those channels may look like). We know the breakout rooms feature can be used to a similar effect, and it may be more useful for temporary groupings. The instructor will usually stay in the main channel or room so that they can respond to student questions. Once a routine is established, overhead times are minimal.

INSTRUCTION

- *How can your facilitation be engaging for all students (regardless of their location)?* In addition to techniques instructors commonly use to create engaging presentations (e.g., class discussion, visual media, humor, inclusion of technology), consider using technological aids such as interactive presentation software (e.g., Mentimeter) and features built into videoconferencing software (e.g., polls, text chat, and reactions). There is research that shows that interactive technology boosts engagement in Synchronous HyFlex settings (Raes et al. 2020).
- *Will every student have access to classroom material?* Consider adding all learning materials, such as classroom videos, handouts, and activity sheets, in predictable places like the classroom LMS or a dedicated discussion forum. This makes it straightforward for students to find what they need.

GENERAL ACTIVITIES

- *How might you ensure every student (remote and F2F) has the opportunity to engage (e.g., ask questions of the instructor, respond to peers)?*

- Creating clear expectations and protocols can enhance classroom participation. For instance, setting the expectation that if remote students raise their hands for questions they will be heard.
- Actively monitoring the classroom chat can encourage remote students to ask questions during the class session.
- Ensuring clear audio so that remote students can hear their face-to-face peers (and vice versa) ensures that students feel involved in the classroom.
- Splitting your attention for orchestrating both modalities can be difficult. Consider delegating responsibilities for certain tasks, such as monitoring the chat, to your students or a teaching assistant.

- *Will students be able to follow along with instruction?* Sharing your screen, narrating your actions, and using visual cues like slides or diagrams helps students follow along.

TEAM-BASED ACTIVITIES

- *How will you provide clear instructions and expectations for online collaboration?* Collaborating over shared documents and communicating (e.g., making announcements) the via group chat features of your team collaboration software (e.g., Microsoft Teams) can help to ensure that everyone is on the same page.
- *Will everyone be able to perform classroom activities?* Transitioning from physical to digital activities when possible can create default activities that are accessible to remote and face-to-face students.
- *How will blended groups effectively communicate?* Providing default spaces in the collaborative software for long term groups (span multiple class periods) can help students meet. See the section on "How to Set Up and Use Your Collaboration Software" for more information.
- *How will you monitor blended groups?* In the physical classroom, walking over and checking in with groups who have remote members can help troubleshoot problems directly. Asking probing questions such as *Are remote students being heard?* can trigger students to take more ownership of their groups' collaboration.
- *Will groups distribute work equitably?* Checking in with groups to ensure that every member is meaningfully contributing is important in any classroom, and even more so in a HyFlex classroom. If student teams are having difficulty communicating in the blended environment, this additional tension may be detrimental to their course performance. Checking in can be as simple as asking questions (e.g.,

How is everyone distributing responsibilities?). Other tools that we use include peer evaluation tools such as CATME (https://info.catme.org/), where groups can rate their members on key metrics and provide qualitative feedback.

SUPPORT

- *How can support be made accessible to all students?* Offering support for both remote and face-to-face students is important for all the same reasons we employ Interactive Synchronous HyFlex in our teaching: accessibility and equity. One obvious way to offer support is to make your office hours available to both remote and face-to-face students. Another perhaps less common way is to create spaces for support through the collaboration software (e.g., a "questions" channel on Teams) or other discussion forum software. Anecdotally, many of our instructors are more responsive to student queries on Microsoft Teams and believe it allows for faster, more casual communication (and, so far, it's free of spam messages). Instant messaging on Teams may feel less formal than email, letting students engage in easier back-and-forth for small questions that they may otherwise hesitate to ask.

QUICK TIP 	How to Create Office Hour Appointments
	We use Microsoft Bookings or Calendly to set up our calendars to let students make appointments for either face-to-face or remote meetings. Other tools like YouCanBookMe or Google Appointments can also be useful. Once you create your meeting link, post the link in several places where students are likely to see it (e.g., syllabus, LMS home page, instructor email signature).

RESEARCH SPOTLIGHT 	Can Deep Learning Thrive in HyFlex Environments?
	See chapter 5 for details. Refer to Study 6 for preliminary findings on deep learning outcomes in HyFlex versus traditional face-to-face settings.

RESEARCH SPOTLIGHT 	How Does Blended Group Composition Affect Team Performance in HyFlex? *See chapter 5 for details.* Refer to Study 8 to understand the academic success of teams in HyFlex environments, considering the impact of blending remote and face-to-face members on group performance.

REFERENCES

Elen, Jan. 2020. "'Instructional Disobedience': A Largely Neglected Phenomenon Deserving More Systematic Research Attention." *Educational Technology Research and Development* 68 (5): 2021–32. https://doi.org/10.1007/s11423-020-09776-3.

Garrison, D. Randy, and Norman D. Vaughan. 2008. *Blended Learning in Higher Education: Framework, Principles, and Guidelines.* John Wiley & Sons.

Kirschner, Paul A., and Jeroen J. G. van Merriënboer. 2013. "Do Learners Really Know Best? Urban Legends in Education." *Educational Psychologist* 48 (3): 169–83. https://doi.org/10.1080/00461520.2013.804395.

Raes, Annelies, Pieter Vanneste, Marieke Pieters, Ine Windey, Wim Van Den Noortgate, and Fien Depaepe. 2020. "Learning and Instruction in the Hybrid Virtual Classroom: An Investigation of Students' Engagement and the Effect of Quizzes." *Computers & Education* 143 (January):103682. https://doi.org/10.1016/j.compedu.2019.103682.

3

FACILITATING INTERACTIVE SYNCHRONOUS HYFLEX CLASSROOMS

This chapter guides you through the final days before your course begins and the day-to-day flow once it's underway. The chapter is organized into four parts:

1. Final preparations for the semester
2. Navigating the first days of class
3. Maintaining daily interactions
4. Supporting students after class

We begin with a quick checklist to help with readiness, offering practical advice on classroom setup for Interactive Synchronous HyFlex and practicing your instruction. Next, we explore how to start your classes on the right note by establishing clear norms and fostering a sense of community among your students. As your classes progress, we offer strategies to maintain this momentum. Finally, we provide suggestions on how to effectively support your students whenever challenges or needs arise.

PART 1: FINAL PREPARATIONS FOR THE SEMESTER

In chapter 2 we discussed preparation and how to set up for your classroom. In this chapter we share a checklist you can use to ensure that you are ready and practiced for what is often an exciting and slightly anxious first day of class. The strategies discussed in this section directly align with establishing meaningful teaching presence, a key component of the Community of Inquiry (CoI) framework. Specifically, the design and organization methods instructors use relate to how they provide instructions for participation, navigate the course, and provide course information and examples to help establish an effective community.

ENSURING A SMOOTH START

Remember, Interactive Synchronous HyFlex is based on the design principle of low overhead. With the exception of a conferencing microphone, you likely have most of the hardware you will need to get started (see the section "Low Overhead: Getting Started Is Easy" in chapter 1). A little planning can go a long way to make sure you're ready. Ask yourself the following questions:

- *Are students prepared for the first day?* Students need to be aware of your expectations for the first session (like to bring their laptops!). See the section "Design Principles of the Interactive Synchronous HyFlex Model" in chapter 1 for our Day 1 requirements. Once in the classroom, you can reinforce and provide additional instruction to help them get ready for the term, such as expectations for Interactive Synchronous HyFlex.

FIGURE 3.1 In this section, we provide a quick checklist to make sure you're ready for your first day. The checklist in the image may be based on experience. SOURCE: Abdul Moeed Asad (Co-author)

FACILITATING INTERACTIVE SYNCHRONOUS HYFLEX CLASSROOMS / 51

EXAMPLE

Sharing Expectations for Quality Engagement

We share expectations as a set of introduction announcements and reminders through the LMS. We also embed expectations in other locations, including the course syllabus. During the first few class sessions, we review classroom expectations as part of the in-class seminar.

- *Have you set up your learning management system (LMS) with the necessary information?* Important information includes the syllabus, classroom session and assignment information, and tutorials on how to use and troubleshoot classroom software. See the checklist below for the things you could include.
- *How will students gain access to the collaboration software?* You can invite students via direct invites or provide instructions for joining the software on the LMS (e.g., we provide our students with a Microsoft Teams join code and expect them to join as part of class preparation). Additionally, you can set up any orientation material on the collaboration software as well (such as introducing yourself). These strategies promote social presence, a key component of the CoI framework. For additional instructions on how to use the LMS and collaboration software, see the section "Setting Up the Classroom Environment for Interactive Synchronous HyFlex" in chapter 2.

CHECKLIST FOR INTERACTIVE SYNCHRONOUS HYFLEX		
	ITEM/TASK	COMMENTS
✓	Syllabus with HyFlex expectations	Expectations related to HyFlex: include your attendance or participation policy for both face-to-face and remote participation.
✓	Contact information for staff, including the instructor and, if applicable and desired, the teaching assistant and other relevant resources	Knowing who to contact can help students reach out in case they may be struggling to, e.g., join the collaboration software, especially on the first day of class.

CHECKLIST FOR INTERACTIVE SYNCHRONOUS HYFLEX *(continued)*

	ITEM/TASK	COMMENTS
✓	Invitation to the collaboration software	An easy way to invite students is to include an invitation link to the collaboration software (such as Microsoft Teams). This approach (versus manually inviting students) is helpful at the start of the semester when lots of students may be adding and dropping a course.
✓	Set up a recurring meeting or individual meetings	Recurring meeting links use the same link every time and reduce setup effort. You could share the meeting link once prominently on the LMS and your collaboration software and never have to set it up again. However, individual meetings also have their advantages. See the Fine Print box below for an example of a workflow that uses individual meetings.
✓	Preparation assignment information (if any)	To hit the ground running, we have students download and install Microsoft Teams and post an introduction of themselves on Teams to get familiar with the interface (and their new friends).
✓	Walk-through and tutorials (optional)	We include a video tutorial for how to join and use Microsoft Teams. This helps reduce technical issues for students.

THE FINE PRINT

A Use Case for Individual Meetings

One of our instructors uses individual meetings in Microsoft Teams for organizational reasons. They set up their meeting a day before their class session, and it shows up as a post. They title the meeting with a unique name (e.g., "Meeting 3: The Design Process"), which helps them and their students to identify the topic of the day. After the meeting, the meeting's discussions and recordings show up as replies under the main post. This feature is valuable to the instructor and students because it helps users quickly look up content.

RESEARCH SPOTLIGHT 	What Is the Onboarding Experience Like for New HyFlex Instructors?
	See chapter 5 for details.
	Refer to Study 11 to explore the lived experiences of new instructors implementing the Interactive Synchronous HyFlex model.

PRACTICE BUILDS CONFIDENCE AND COMPETENCE

Doing a dry run of the class will help you gain familiarity with moving between modalities and with the software you will be using. We want to emphasize the importance of practice, because practicing can help prevent technical problems during crucial class time. If possible, we recommend simulating remote attendance by asking friends to log into the collaboration software to emulate remote attendance. We recommend running your practice session (e.g., of your first session) in the classroom you will be teaching in to most closely mirror your eventual experience. If you are interested in research, practicing these tasks aligns well with the Technological Pedagogical Content Knowledge (TPACK) framework, which helps instructors effectively respond to technology-enhanced teaching in the classroom.

THE FINE PRINT 	What is TPACK?
	The TPACK (Technological Pedagogical Content Knowledge) framework highlights the intersection of three primary domains: content knowledge (subject matter understanding), pedagogical knowledge (methods and processes of teaching and learning), and technological knowledge (proficiency in technologies) necessary for effective teaching. A comprehensive understanding of these three domains enables teachers to design and implement effective, technology-enhanced experiences (Koehler and Mishra 2009). Recently, the authors updated their framework by revising the contextual component and introducing contextual knowledge (knowledge about the educational environment) as a fourth domain. They emphasized that understanding context is important for effectively applying TPACK in specific situations (Petko et al. 2025). See https://tpack.org/ for further information.

Following are some mechanical and engagement tasks we recommend practicing.

MECHANICAL TASKS

- Set up (or schedule) a meeting in your collaboration software.
- Join the meeting and start recording.
- Share your screen with the room monitor/projector and remote audience.
- Check to make sure that your sound and the sound of media you may want to share is audible in the room and to remote students.

QUICK TIP

Get the Most Audio from Classroom Discussions

Check to see if you have noise suppression features on your device. While these features can be great at isolating a singular main voice in a small group format, they can sometimes cancel classroom discussion voices, especially those at a distance from the microphone, denying the opportunity for remote students to hear those at a distance from the microphone or who speak more softly.

THE FINE PRINT

Do I Need Specialized Equipment?

Investing in equipment such as headphones and external microphones can help to boost the quality of the overall experience. We have had success with the Jabra Speak 750 speaker puck for instructors or as a loaner to small groups for use at their tables. However, don't be afraid to start small.

ENGAGEMENT TASKS

- Practice navigating between face-to-face and remote conversations to avoid favoring one over the other. For instance, start a discussion with face-to-face students, then intentionally switch attention to remote students by asking them a direct question. Alternate who gets to speak first in different segments to balance engagement.
- Become familiar with using the announcement and chat features to address students in both modalities. An illustrative task is to post a quick discussion question in the chat. Observe the time it takes for all students to formulate their responses.

- Practice any other key feature that makes sense for your classroom. In our classroom we transition from a whole class discussion to small blended groups. For such a transition, practice could mean moving into small group discussion with a second device (such as a phone) to check in on groups.

Overall, consider how you would like to establish your instructor presence modalities, then intentionally practice strategies that support your approach.

PART 2: NAVIGATING THE FIRST DAYS OF CLASS

In the initial days of class, we want to set the tone and establish norms for Interactive Synchronous HyFlex environments. In this section, we offer some practical advice on how to make students feel welcome and ensure that they are familiar with and accustomed to the Interactive Synchronous HyFlex format. The strategies discussed align with social presence, a core element of the CoI framework. Instructors can use affective strategies (e.g., sharing a video or images on their screen, introducing themself, sharing values), cohesive strategies (e.g., greeting students both face-to-face and remote by using their names; creating collaborative activities that engage both face-to-face and remote students), and open communication strategies (e.g., acknowledging students' ideas across modalities, prompting participation that is accessible to both face-to-face and remote students). (See figure 3.2.)

FIGURE 3.2 As HyFlex instructors, we are mindful to be present and audible for our students across modalities by positioning ourselves in front of the classroom camera and speaking into a speaker puck (or our laptop's mic).
SOURCE: Abdul Moeed Asad (Co-author)

RELATED SECTION 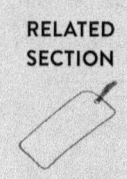	**Forming a Community** We use the CoI framework to ground our work. Refer to the section "Developing Expectations for Meaningful Interactions" in chapter 2 for more information.

QUICK TIP 	**Are Your Norms Inclusive?** Dr. Brian Beatty, the person who coined the term "HyFlex" and an experienced HyFlex educator, shared that it can be difficult to move beyond the idea that remote students could be learning better if they were face-to-face. This belief may act as a crutch, helping us to normalize not supporting remote students in ways that help them learn their best (instead of doing the work). You can see Dr. Beatty's work at https://edtechbooks.org/hyflex/teaching_hyflex.

1. ESTABLISH YOUR PRESENCE TO BUILD RAPPORT AND MODEL BEHAVIOR

We believe students should feel comfortable interacting with both their peers and their instructors, and the presence an instructor establishes can help to create a comfortable learning environment for students. As instructors, we can model interactions for students to follow. Watching us do these activities can help familiarize students with the tools available to them and how to effectively use them. Here are some things we can do in class and on the collaboration software:

- Share a bit about ourselves, including our background and interests (as shown in figure 3.3). Additionally, personal stories can help humanize us and make us seem approachable. Disclosing personal information and values aligns with the affective domain of social presence in the CoI framework.
- Have students become familiar with each other. We can use icebreakers to help students get to know each other and feel more comfortable in the classroom. In the example that follows, we share what that might look like in an Interactive Synchronous HyFlex classroom.
- Narrate while we're screen sharing. This helps students follow along.

EXAMPLE 	**A Simple Icebreaker Activity**
	At the start of the semester, we have students introduce themselves using the chat feature of the collaboration software (for us, Microsoft Teams). We have them share their name, their major, where they're from, and why they joined the university. We also have students greet each other on these posts. This process helps them become accustomed to the software and get to know their peers.
	Instructors also share introductions using the collaboration software as a way to model behavior.

- Engage with the classroom chat and discussion forums to model active participation.
- Engage with both face-to-face and remote students to demonstrate that all participants are valued.
- Keep the instructor's webcam turned on. This helps students feel more connected and encourages them to do the same.
- Provide clear instructions on how to navigate the HyFlex environment (e.g., *If you're remote, please start a meeting in your group channel.*).

Welcome to TECH120!

I'm Moeed and I'll be your instructor for TECH120. I thought I'd send a message here to introduce myself and the course tools.

About me
Since this is Purdue, you might find it unsurprising that I have a STEM background. I'm a computer scientist turned designer from Lahore, Pakistan. I'm a second/final year user experience graduate student and this will be my third (and likely last) time teaching TECH120. In my free time, I enjoy watching food (nothing that I will make) and architecture videos (nothing that I can afford).

Contact: Get in touch if you have questions or feedback about how the course is going. Send me a message here on teams (fastest way to get to me usually), email - ▮▮▮▮▮▮▮▮ or come to my help hours https://calendly.com/▮▮▮▮▮▮▮▮▮▮▮▮ (these can be remote or in-person).

FIGURE 3.3 You can introduce yourself and link to important information in your first message to your students. SOURCE: Abdul Moeed Asad (Co-author)

2. FOSTERING COMMUNITY ACROSS MODALITIES

In an Interactive Synchronous HyFlex classroom, we aim to foster a sense of community between students whether they are remote or face-to-face. Cultivating a sense of community can motivate students to engage deeply with one another and the course content. Here are some tips to cultivate community:

- Encourage students to keep their webcams on and communicate why this is important. According to research (Meishar-Tal and Forkosh-Baruch 2022), facial expressions communicate important cues for understanding (e.g., agreement or confusion) and seeing others' faces can help build familiarity with peers. Furthermore, having cameras turned on promotes strong social presence, a key to creating a meaningful community of inquiry.
- If your classroom includes active time in groups, monitor group interactions to ensure that no students are being excluded based on their modality. Move around the room, particularly to blended groups, and ask groups if everyone is able to participate and how they're dividing responsibilities. If you notice any issues, you can provide guidance to promote inclusive engagement.

RESEARCH SPOTLIGHT

How Is Instructor Presence Established in HyFlex Classrooms?

See chapter 5 for details.

Refer to Study 10 to investigate how instructor presence is established in HyFlex classrooms and whether variations in instructor approaches are associated with student perceptions of instructor presence.

---

3. THINK ABOUT ACCESSIBILITY

One primary advantage of HyFlex is increased accessibility, as we discuss (and the literature on HyFlex supports) in chapter 1 in the section "Why Consider Implementing HyFlex Classrooms?" Interactive Synchronous HyFlex classrooms are fundamentally more accessible due to the flexibility they offer, enabling more students that are unable to physically attend class to participate. For example, a student who is ill with a mild contagious infection can attend remotely, and

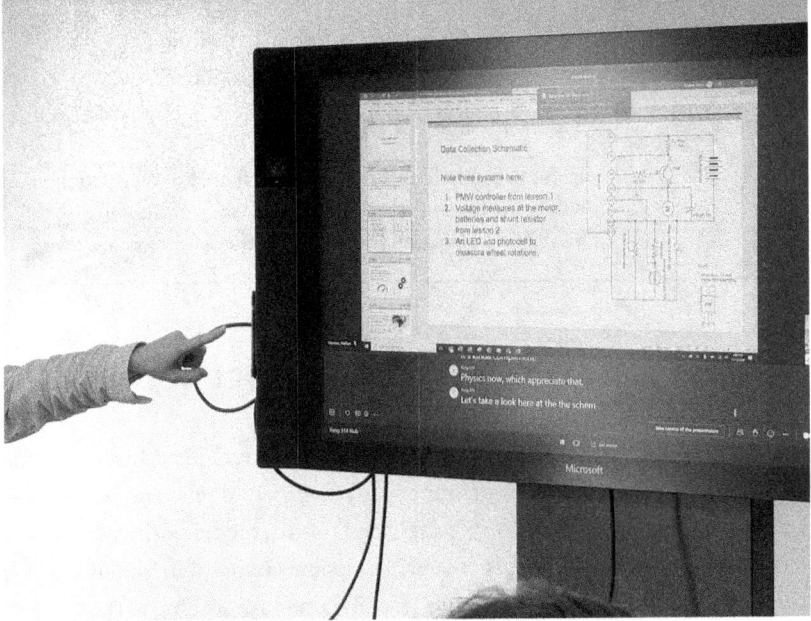

FIGURE 3.4 Instructors can turn on captions on their devices to model the feature to students. SOURCE: Abdul Moeed Asad (Co-author)

students unable to come to class can use class recordings as instructional material to help them make up their work. Recordings also allow students attending a class session to revisit content, which can be helpful to support students' study outside of class and non-native English speakers.

Beyond this flexibility, collaboration software that enables Synchronous HyFlex classrooms has a list of accessibility features. Modeling and explaining these accessibility features to students in the class can be beneficial (as shown in figure 3.4). Here are a few features we use regularly and how they may help students:

- *Screen sharing:* Helps those with visual impairments and/or those seated far from the class projection screen.
- *Live captioning:* Helps those with hearing disabilities and/or those far from the speaker and non-native speakers.
- *Chat threads:* Helps those who might have anxiety, are introverted, and/or otherwise prefer texting.

RESEARCH SPOTLIGHT 	**Does HyFlex Enhance Learning for Students with Disabilities?** *See chapter 5 for details.* Refer to Study 12 to determine whether HyFlex instruction enhances the learning and performance of students with disabilities compared to students without accommodations.

PART 3: MAINTAINING DAILY INTERACTIONS

Once norms are established, except the occasional technical hiccup or student confusion, Interactive Synchronous HyFlex classrooms tend to function smoothly. Continuing to enforce established norms, model positive behaviors, and adapt to the evolving needs of your classroom is important. Simultaneously, these practices help establish effective teaching presence, leading to the development of an effective community of inquiry. Following are some tips and reminders to help maintain a conducive learning environment.

RELATED SECTION 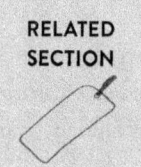	**Troubleshooting and More** See chapter 6 for more on troubleshooting and improving your teaching practice.

KICKING OFF CLASS

Developing a kickoff routine for class is very important. This can include setting up the computer, checking the audiovisual system, and opening any material that will be used in the classroom. We suggest these minor additions to your routine:

- *Reinforce norms:* Occasionally, and as necessary (perhaps after large gaps such as holiday breaks, or if many students seem to be needing assistance), remind students of your expectations. For example, some instructors from our group ask remote students to indicate they are present by typing "hi" in

the chat. After a break, reminding students to continue this practice can be helpful (e.g., *Please remember to say hi in the chat if you're remote.*).
- *Record sessions:* When feasible and policy-appropriate, record your large group instruction. This helps absent students catch up and allows everyone to revisit material. Also, it's an easy way to reduce the number of times you will hear students ask, *What did I miss?*

DURING CLASS FACILITATION

As you go about class, we recommend being mindful of the following:

- *Invite inclusive participation:* Ensure that you are engaging both remote and face-to-face students. You can direct certain questions to your remote students, encouraging them to speak up and signaling that you value their contribution. Additionally, using tools (e.g., Google Docs) that facilitate easy participation regardless of modality can support all students.
- *Facilitate HyFlex interactions:* Periodically check in with blended groups or remote students as they go about their tasks. For example, a simple *Can our remote friends hear us?* addressed to a blended group can go a long way in making remote students feel supported and heard.

TOOLKIT FOR TROUBLESHOOTING

We will talk more about troubleshooting in chapter 6, "Troubleshooting and Improving Your Interactive Synchronous HyFlex Instruction." However, here are things that may be of immediate concern:

- *Enlist help:* Orchestrating two modalities in the classroom can be a tenuous task in Synchronous HyFlex classrooms. The larger the classroom, the more complex it can become to facilitate learning. If you do not have assistance (e.g., a teaching assistant to help), you can lessen this burden by empowering your students to facilitate and troubleshoot with you in the classroom.
- *Encourage personal accountability:* Some students may make choices that are not in their best interest (e.g., a student who is struggling in class and chooses to regularly attend class remotely). Asking students to reflect (e.g., *Is remote attendance helping you succeed? Let's figure out a plan that works better for you.*) can help them make changes and better choices.

PART 4: SUPPORTING STUDENTS AFTER CLASS

We have discussed various ways to design support for HyFlex classrooms. These are aligned with specific CoI strategies aimed at offering support in navigating course structure, using course resources to make sense of content, and receiving tips for successfully participating in the course. The following are some tried and tested ideas.

SUPPORT RESOURCES

Creating support resources in the LMS for central software used in the classroom can save time for both students and instructors. In a busy classroom, have students reference the support section before contacting the teaching staff. We talk more about this in the section "How to Configure Your LMS to Support HyFlex Environments" in chapter 2.

CLASSROOM RECORDINGS

Sometimes students will find it helpful to review what happened in the classroom. There can be multiple reasons for doing so, the most obvious being absence. Other reasons include reviewing an important discussion in the classroom or capturing their group's presentation. Playback controls such as setting the speed of play and closed-captioning make reviewing material online an efficient experience.

METHODS OF COMMUNICATION

In the Interactive Synchronous HyFlex classroom, we encourage the instructors to offer office hours both face-to-face and remotely. As a reminder, we use Microsoft Teams, which offers features that allow students to book meetings. You can also use other solutions such as YouCanBookMe, Calendly, or Google Appointments to do the same.

Additionally, many instructors on our team use Microsoft Teams to respond to personal messages, quickly answering student queries. The mode of direct messaging may be more casual, allowing for easier back-and-forth for small questions—questions students might hesitate to ask via email.

REFERENCES

Koehler, Matthew J., and Punya Mishra. (2009). "What Is Technological Pedagogical Content Knowledge?" *Contemporary Issues in Technology and Teacher Education*, 9 (1). https://citejournal.org/volume-9/issue-1-09/general/what-is-technological-pedagogicalcontent-knowledge.

Meishar-Tal, Hagit, and Alona Forkosh-Baruch. 2022. "'Now You See Me, Now You Don't': Why Students Avoid Turning on Their Cameras in Synchronous Online Lessons?" *Interactive Learning Environments* 32 (5): 1737–50. https://doi.org/10.1080/10494820.2022.2127778.

Petko, Dominik, Punya Mishra, and Matthew J. Koehler. 2025. "TPACK in Context: An Updated Model." *Computers and Education Open* 8 (June): 100244. https://doi.org/10.1016/j.caeo.2025.100244.

4
HYFLEX VIGNETTES

This chapter is about transfer. While the majority of this book is based on research and experience in one large introductory college level design thinking course, we envision that the utility of the Interactive Synchronous HyFlex principles is not limited to this one course. We use this course as a context because it is large, serving nearly fourteen hundred students annually through sections of forty students each. Thus, insights shared previously come from a synthesis of many instructors, thousands of student experiences, and five years of funded research. Though we find confidence in this sturdy backdrop, in this chapter we share our reflections of a transfer of the HyFlex approach (to five other Purdue courses across four vignettes taught by the authors of this text:

FIGURE 4.1 This chapter is about successful transfers of Interactive Synchronous HyFlex to other contexts.
SOURCE: Abdul Moeed Asad (Co-author)

1. EDCI 558: Methods of Teaching Integrated STEM (Secondary Education)
2. TLI 361: Engineering and Technology Education Instructional Planning and Evaluation; TLI 262: Foundations of Integrated STEM Education
3. EDCI 490: Engineering by Design—Elementary
4. EPICS 039: EPICS (Engineering Projects in Community Service)

VIGNETTES

VIGNETTE 1: EDCI 558, METHODS OF TEACHING INTEGRATED STEM (SECONDARY EDUCATION)

QUICK LOOK	
COURSE LEVEL	Graduate
COURSE TYPE	Mandatory
ENROLLMENT	Medium-sized classroom—15 to 30 students
TEACHING STYLES	Active learning with some lectures; experiential, team-based
INSTRUCTION NOTES	Team-taught with two faculty representing two STEM disciplines
SPECIAL EQUIPMENT	Employs a Jabra Speak 750 speaker puck for improved audio quality in whole group discussions

EDCI 558, a methods of teaching course, is a requirement of the certificate for graduate and undergraduate students in secondary integrated STEM. As a methods course, students practice teaching in class and have a field experience where they teach in a public school classroom. This course has been offered once a year, as HyFlex, since fall 2020 and typically draws enrollment of fifteen to thirty students. Undergraduates are usually in their final semester prior to student teaching, and graduate students are typically former teachers, future teachers, or future faculty. To support authenticity in the STEM disciplines, this course is team-taught by two faculty representing two of the STEM disciplines.

This course meets once per week, in the evening, for a duration of three hours and is heavily active learning with sporadic brief episodes of lecture. Most students live off campus, with some commuting an hour or more. Conference travel, treacherous winter road conditions, and seasonal flu impact the ability of students

FIGURE 4.2 Two instructors navigate team teaching. The required equipment for this classroom is a laptop connected to a HDMI and a speaker puck to capture the audio in the room. We turn off software based noise cancellation to better capture everyone's voice. SOURCE: Abdul Moeed Asad (Co-author)

to participate face-to-face. These same realities of academic life impact the faculty's ability to participate consistently face-to-face as well.

The course is categorized as face-to-face in the registration catalog. On the first evening of class, via the learning management software (LMS) and in the syllabus, we stress to students that discussions and participation are easier, and richer, face-to-face. We then encourage them to participate remotely if they are unable to be in the classroom physically. Students often message the instructor if they expect to be remote, which is convenient but not strictly necessary. When students do alert their instructor, the instructor can help facilitate connecting students in the room with their peers and make sure remote students can hear, see, and contribute.

Typical routines in class include an instructor-led orientation and a brief lecture, and student discussion in small table groups (see figure 4.2), often with

FIGURE 4.3 Students communicate with the remote instructor on Teams. SOURCE: Abdul Moeed Asad (Co-author)

whole group reporting out. The foundation of the course is service-learning, such that teams are assigned a local teacher as a client, and they develop and teach a curriculum unit for their classroom. This partnership requires extensive communication with the partner teacher, which is often facilitated remotely.

The lead instructor created a team in Microsoft Teams for the course and manually added students to the team. A recurring meeting was scheduled in the general channel of the course team, and the link to the team, recurring meeting, and recordings are posted in the LMS for students to access. As the teams of students work regularly with their clients and each other, a separate channel is created for each team, and students know they will meet in that channel for small group work. Thus, when students or local client teachers or instructors participate remotely, they start by joining the recurring meeting in the general channel (as shown in figure 4.3). When we transition to small groups, students launch a meeting in their team channel. We frequently oscillate between the whole group and small groups, and students jump between the two active meetings. The whole group typically offers better audio because the instructor uses a conference room speaker puck (Jabra Speak 750) and shares discussion prompts on slides, while the small group meetings foster table-level discussions. Students often join the meeting in the classroom to make viewing the shared screen easier, depending on where they are seated.

VIGNETTE 2: TLI 361, ENGINEERING AND TECHNOLOGY EDUCATION INSTRUCTIONAL PLANNING AND EVALUATION; AND TLI 262, FOUNDATIONS OF INTEGRATED STEM EDUCATION

QUICK LOOK	
COURSE LEVEL	Undergraduate
COURSE TYPE	Required for preservice teachers
ENROLLMENT	Small classroom—11 students in TLI 361, 6 students in TLI 262
TEACHING STYLES	Lecture, discussion, reflection, paired group work
INSTRUCTION NOTES	Taught by one instructor; classes meet twice per week
SPECIAL EQUIPMENT	Uses a Microsoft Teams Room hub with camera, microphone, and large monitor

TLI 361 and TLI 262 are required for undergraduate preservice teachers. In the TLI 361 course, students are exposed to a breadth of K–12 curricula available in their field. They critically analyze a selected curriculum and culminate their learning experience by creating a curriculum of their own design. In the TLI 262 course, students are engaged in readings and course projects to promote understanding of integrated STEM education in practice. The courses meet twice weekly for seventy-five minutes. The courses were taught as HyFlex for the first time in the spring and fall of 2024 with eleven (TLI 316) and six students (TLI 262) who live on or near campus.

Similar to the previously described course, this is a face-to-face course in the registration system that affords remote participation as needed. The class met in a classroom that had a Microsoft Teams Room hub with a camera, microphone, and large monitor (see figure 4.4). Using Microsoft Teams, a recurring meeting was scheduled (and recording was automatically triggered when the meeting was started) using the same link each time. Students were expected to be in the classroom when possible and typically were remote when they were feeling sick. In cases where students were traveling or too sick to participate synchronously, they would watch the recording to catch up on missed material and then engage in an alternative assignment if relevant. In the LMS, students were provided with three links: one for the recurring meeting, one for recordings, and one link to the Teams general channel so they could communicate with their peers or post files for sharing (as shown in figure 4.5).

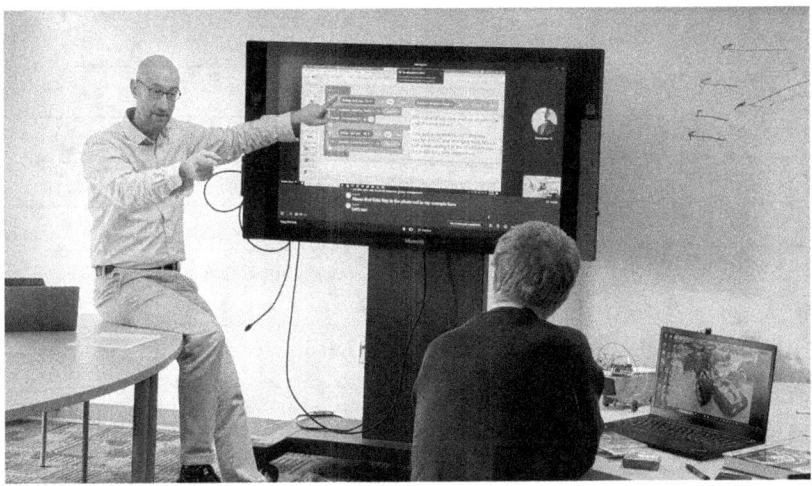

FIGURE 4.4 HyFlex is useful in traditional classrooms to help record, transcribe, and caption meetings. The specialized equipment (Microsoft Teams Room Hub) can make setup simple. SOURCE: Abdul Moeed Asad (Co-author)

FIGURE 4.5 Students can easily share their own work by using screen sharing (the screen is being shared from the student on the right's laptop). SOURCE: Abdul Moeed Asad (Co-author)

Learning experiences included lecture, discussion, reflection, and paired group work. As learning was primarily at the whole group level, the general channel recurring class meeting was typically the only meeting needed. The instructor and, as needed, students joined the meeting to share screens for presentations.

VIGNETTE 3: EDCI 490, ENGINEERING BY DESIGN—ELEMENTARY

QUICK LOOK	
COURSE LEVEL	Undergraduate
COURSE TYPE	Option for elementary integrated STEM certificate
ENROLLMENT	Small classroom—3 to 5 students
TEACHING STYLES	Lecture, student presentations, active learning (lab time for design and building)
INSTRUCTION NOTES	Team-taught by a university faculty member and a classroom teacher who co-teaches remotely from another state
SPECIAL EQUIPMENT	Uses a Microsoft Teams Room hub with camera, microphone, and large monitor

EDCI 490, a methods of teaching course, is one way to satisfy a requirement of the certificate for undergraduate students in elementary integrated STEM. As a methods course, students practice teaching in class and have a field experience where they teach in a public school classroom. Since 2020, this course has been offered once or twice a year as HyFlex and typically draws enrollment of three to five students to satisfy a scholarship grant requirement. Undergraduates are usually in their final year prior to student teaching. This course is team-taught by a university faculty member and a classroom teacher who co-teaches remotely from another state (see figure 4.6).

This course meeting pattern is modeled after typical teacher professional development workshops such that we meet during larger blocks of time on a few evenings during the semester. While the small class of students typically meets face-to-face, travel or sickness occasionally (but very rarely) necessitates students participating remotely. Because she resides in another state, the classroom teacher who co-teaches the class participates remotely for each class meeting.

Similar to the previous two course descriptions, this course is categorized as face-to-face in the registration catalog. On the first evening of class, in the LMS and in the syllabus, we share with students that discussions and participation are easier, and richer, face-to-face. We then encourage them to participate remotely if they are unable to be in the classroom physically. Students often message the instructor if they expect to be absent, which is convenient but not strictly necessary. The LMS includes a link to the course recordings and the general channel, which is where the meetings are started.

FIGURE 4.6 The classroom has a simple setup that uses a chromebook set at a high vantage point as an additional camera. This camera lets the remote instructor view the whole classroom. SOURCE: Abdul Moeed Asad (Co-author)

Typical routines in class include instructor-led presentations on key contents of the course, student presentations, and lab time to design and build. To prepare for each meeting, the instructor positions an old Chromebook in a corner of the classroom and joins the class meeting with the camera on and the mic disabled. Then, the instructor connects their computer to the meeting with a Jabra speaker puck at the center of the large table where everyone sits (as shown in figure 4.7). By toggling the camera on and off from the instructor's computer, the remote co-teacher can see a close-up of the face-to-face co-instructor's face or a wide-angle shot of the classroom. Students are asked to join the meeting with their cameras on and audio muted, which results in the remote co-instructor having a close-up view of each student's face, making facial expressions easy to read. The co-instructor's camera is highlighted in the Microsoft Teams system, making it larger on each student's screen, thereby making the co-instructors' presentation and facial expressions especially visible. While working in the lab or during brief field trips, the faculty member on campus transitions the call to their phone and carries the co-instructor around the lab or outside the classroom.

FIGURE 4.7 Face-to-face and remote instructors team teach while communicating with each other and the students synchronously. SOURCE: Abdul Moeed Asad (Co-author)

VIGNETTE 4: EPICS 039 (ENGINEERING PROJECTS IN COMMUNITY SERVICE)

QUICK LOOK	
COURSE LEVEL	Undergraduate
COURSE TYPE	Optional
ENROLLMENT	Medium classroom—22 students
TEACHING STYLES	Highly student-led with guidance from instructors; weekly student presentations
INSTRUCTION NOTES	Connects Purdue's West Lafayette campus with its Indianapolis location; co-taught by advisors from both locations, with support from teaching assistants
SPECIAL EQUIPMENT	High-quality cameras and audio systems for seamless interaction

FIGURE 4.8 The classroom is set up to facilitate capture of HyFlex meetings. A camera captures the entire class while the screen is shared via the share screen feature on Microsoft Teams. SOURCE: Abdul Moeed Asad (Co-author)

This EPICS (Engineering Projects in Community Service) course exemplifies Purdue University's commitment to innovative, student-led learning experiences. Offered as a HyFlex model, it connects Purdue's West Lafayette campus with its merged Indianapolis location (see figures 4.8 and 4.9), a union that occurred in the fall of 2024. The course attracts students from various engineering disciplines at both undergraduate and graduate levels, fostering interdisciplinary collaboration and community engagement.

The course is co-taught by advisors at both locations, with additional support from teaching assistants (TAs) at each campus. This team of instructors facilitates a highly student-led learning environment, guiding rather than directing the project work. The HyFlex model has proven crucial in maintaining the course's collaborative nature across the two campuses.

Class sessions follow a unique structure designed to maximize student leadership and cross-campus interaction. Each week begins with student team presentations, a cornerstone of the EPICS program. Teams report on their weekly progress, discuss challenges, and outline goals for the coming week. The HyFlex setup, utilizing Microsoft Teams, allows students from both locations to actively participate in these presentations, ensuring that all voices are heard regardless of physical location (see figure 4.10).

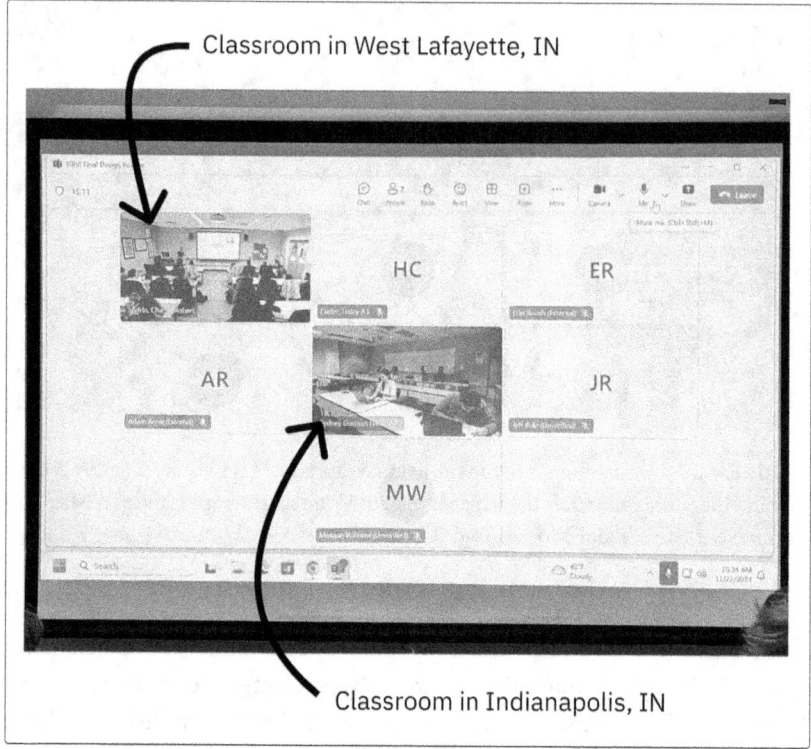

FIGURE 4.9 The EPICS program connects Purdue's West Lafayette (WL) campus with its Indianapolis location. SOURCE: Abdul Moeed Asad (Co-author)

Given that the project is a continuation from previous semesters, most of the hardware and software resources are located at the West Lafayette campus. The HyFlex model has been instrumental in overcoming this potential barrier. Students at the Indianapolis location can visually inspect hardware through video feeds and participate in real-time troubleshooting sessions. Microsoft Teams serves as more than just a videoconferencing tool. It's a hub for quick video calls between smaller project groups, enabling Indianapolis students to collaborate closely with their West Lafayette counterparts on hardware-specific tasks.

Microsoft Teams channels have become a central collaborative space for the course. Students continuously update shared folders within these channels, housing project documentation, code repositories, and design files. This system allows for asynchronous collaboration and enables instructors and TAs to monitor

FIGURE 4.10 A student in the back of the classroom can use Teams to get a better view of the presentation on display. SOURCE: Abdul Moeed Asad (Co-author)

progress and provide timely feedback without disrupting the student-led nature of the projects (see figure 4.10).

The classrooms at both locations are equipped with cameras and audio systems to facilitate seamless interaction. A main camera captures the presenting team and any physical prototypes, while a secondary wide-angle camera provides a view of the entire classroom, helping remote participants feel more connected to the face-to-face environment.

A unique aspect of this course is its ongoing service-learning partnership with the Indiana School for the Blind and Visually Impaired. Staff members and educators from this school, who serve as our project clients, often join class sessions remotely, providing real-time feedback on student presentations and prototypes. These partners represent the end users who will benefit from our students' accessible design solutions. The HyFlex setup allows these partners to engage fully with students, enriching the service-learning experience even when they cannot be physically present on campus.

The HyFlex model has proven particularly beneficial in light of the recent campus merger. It has allowed the EPICS program to adapt quickly, ensuring that the wealth of experience and resources from the West Lafayette campus can be effectively shared with the Indianapolis location. Simultaneously, it has opened up new perspectives and community connections from the Indianapolis students, enriching the program as a whole.

5

A SYNOPSIS OF INTERACTIVE SYNCHRONOUS HYFLEX RESEARCH

This book is based on the experiences of a large teaching team primarily reflecting on a large introductory design course. Additional insights have been drawn from Interactive Synchronous HyFlex implementations in other smaller courses mentioned in chapter 4. Some of our reflections are institutional knowledge shared in team meetings that resemble something between a new instructor mentoring session and story time at a campfire. Though we believe that reflecting on the insights from five years of practice is valuable, we also have made an effort to formalize what we know and understand through rigorous educational research efforts funded by Purdue University's Provost Office Best Practices in Higher Education grant (2020–2021) and the National Science Foundation Improving Undergraduate STEM Education grant (2110799, 2021–2025).

To establish credibility for our claims in other chapters and entice readers to review publications related to these supporting grants, we share a brief synthesis of twelve of our major efforts below, followed by a sensemaking discussion and implications of the studies. These studies were done by the authors of this text and we cite them as evidence for our claims. However, we note that there is

FIGURE 5.1 In this chapter we attempt to compress 12 studies to give a sense of the research that has informed this work. SOURCE: Abdul Moeed Asad (Co-author)

an extensive body of research beyond these studies and we encourage readers to reach into it. Each of the twelve studies shared here are separate studies (published or in process) and focused on the main introductory design course, which was the context for both grants. As separate studies, each has unique samples and methods that span various points during 2020–2025, with a common thread of HyFlex in an active learning, problem-based course on design thinking. We are proud to share this synthesis, the bulk of which was presented and published at the ASEE 2024 conference in Portland Oregon (Mohandas, Lakshmy, Nathan Mentzer, Adrie Koehler, Elnara Mammadova, and Shawn Farrington. 2024. "A Synthesis of Discoveries Spanning Ten Semesters of HyFlex." In *2024 ASEE Annual Conference & Exposition*).

STUDIES

STUDY 1: MOHANDAS, LAKSHMY. 2022. "THE IMPACT OF INTERACTIVE SYNCHRONOUS HYFLEX MODEL ON STUDENTS' PERCEPTION OF SOCIAL, TEACHING AND COGNITIVE PRESENCE IN A DESIGN THINKING COURSE." PHD DISS., PURDUE UNIVERSITY.

QUICK LOOK	
PURPOSE	To investigate how first-year design thinking students experience the Interactive Synchronous HyFlex model, particularly through the lens of the Community of Inquiry (CoI) framework.
KEY FINDINGS	Students generally reported positive perceptions of teaching presence, social presence, and cognitive presence in the HyFlex environment. This was consistent regardless of how students chose to participate daily (face-to-face or remote). The study found evidence of active student interaction and emotional expression, regardless of how students chose to participate.
RECOMMENDATIONS OR IMPLICATIONS	The study recommends clear communication of expectations, using headsets for engaging all students, implementing collaborative activities designed for mixed-modality groups, and encouraging students to keep cameras on to enhance social presence. Institutions adopting this model should assess software and scalability considerations.
LINK	https://doi.org/10.25394/PGS.20359989.v1

The Mohandas dissertation addressed the significant changes in higher education due to technological advancements and the COVID-19 pandemic, leading to a rise in remote and blended learning. Notably, the HyFlex (hybrid flexible) model has emerged as a new standard, offering benefits such as student choice, equivalency, reusability, and accessibility. Despite its popularity, existing literature on HyFlex highlights technological and pedagogical challenges, particularly in dynamic, group-based courses. This study introduced and examined the Interactive Synchronous HyFlex model, aiming to provide an engaging and equitable classroom experience for students in active group-based classrooms, regardless of their attendance mode.

A convergent parallel mixed methods case study was conducted to understand students' experiences through the lens of the Community of Inquiry (CoI) framework. The central research question was: *How and in what ways do first-year design thinking students experience the Interactive Synchronous HyFlex model through the lens of CoI?* Sub-questions investigated the model's effectiveness for social, cognitive, and teaching presence; variation based on participation mode; and how students' experiences shape their perceptions.

The study's quantitative phase employed the CoI survey, focusing on teaching presence, social presence, and cognitive presence. Descriptive statistics and MANOVA (multivariate analysis of variance) tests were used to assess the model's effectiveness. Results showed a general agreement among students regarding teaching presence, social presence, and cognitive presence elements in the HyFlex environment, irrespective of their daily participation mode choices. The qualitative phase considered students' experiences in the HyFlex design thinking class through focus group interviews, classroom observations, and discussion forums, simultaneously offering data triangulation. The findings revealed active student interaction and emotional expression, regardless of their daily participation mode choices. The study also observed how cognitive presence, teaching presence, and social presence were integrated into class activities through various strategies used by the instructors and students themselves. Using contiguous data integration, key findings showed confirmation coherence across data sources.

Teaching presence was perceived very positively by students, as instructors actively facilitated learning by engaging both remote and face-to-face students using visual aids, collaborative software, and inclusive questioning. Regarding social presence, students openly communicated and expressed emotions regardless of participation mode, and groups demonstrated cohesion during in-class and out-of-class collaborations. Considering cognitive presence, the design thinking projects required exploration, integration, and resolution of ideas, reflecting cognitive presence. However, triggering events designed to motivate participation varied from student to student based on intrinsic interest. Overall, the Interactive Synchronous HyFlex model successfully provided flexible, equitable, and engaging learning with a solid sense of community during a challenging pandemic semester.

Recommendations included evidence-based guidance for effectively designing and implementing a student-centered collaborative HyFlex approach. Specifically, instructors should clearly communicate expectations, use headsets to engage all students, and implement collaborative activities for mixed-modality groups. Students should leverage the flexibility responsibly and keep cameras on for social presence. Assessing appropriate software and scalability considerations for class size and layout are advised at an institutional level when adopting this model. While teaching presence often overshadows other presences (Akyol and Garrison 2008), here they were balanced. Communication barriers common in other HyFlex formats (Kohnke and Moorhouse 2022) were also effectively minimized through instructor strategies and recording of sessions. In conclusion, despite pandemic disruptions, the Interactive Synchronous HyFlex model showed potential for facilitating connected and equitable learning experiences critical for unpredictable circumstances in higher education.

STUDY 2: MOHANDAS, LAKSHMY, NATHAN MENTZER, ADRIE KOEHLER, AND SHAWN FARRINGTON. 2023. "TO BE FACE-TO-FACE TODAY OR TO BE REMOTE TODAY: THAT IS THE QUESTION." IN *PROCEEDINGS OF THE 2023 AERA ANNUAL MEETING*. AERA.

QUICK LOOK	
PURPOSE	To examine student perceptions of a HyFlex model after the initial COVID-19 surge, as learning environments were returning to pre-pandemic norms.
KEY FINDINGS	Students continued to experience positive classroom communities in the Interactive Synchronous HyFlex class, with high scores given for teaching presence, cognitive presence, and social presence. These perceptions were consistent across face-to-face and remote participation modes.
RECOMMENDATIONS OR IMPLICATIONS	The study suggests that HyFlex models can effectively maintain student engagement and a sense of community in blended learning environments during and after the COVID-19 pandemic. The flexibility offered by HyFlex is highlighted as a key factor in addressing challenges like student engagement and Zoom fatigue.
LINK	https://doi.org/10.3102/2017564

Building on the first study by reviewing data a year later, this study by Mohandas et al. (2023) examined students' perceptions of a HyFlex model post-COVID surge. Although learning experiences and environments were returning to pre-pandemic norms, issues like Zoom fatigue were prevalent. Similar to the first study, the CoI framework was used in this study. The CoI framework, aligned with literature on

HyFlex and student-centered learning environments, considers three constructs: teaching presence, social presence, and cognitive presence (Akyol et al. 2009).

In fall 2021, with a return to normal attendance policies, students were asked to complete the CoI survey to gather their perceptions regarding the community quality in the course. Six hundred seventy-four students were enrolled, with a response rate of 62.6% (422 students). Quantitative data analysis, including descriptive statistics and correlation analysis, was used to address the research questions.

Students generally experienced positive classroom communities in the Interactive Synchronous HyFlex class, with high scores in teaching, cognitive, and social presences. Correlation analysis showed that students' perception of these presences was similar regardless of how often students chose to participate remotely. The study indicated that in a HyFlex learning environment, students' sense of classroom community was not affected by their daily choice of class participation mode. This supports the use of HyFlex models in the peri-pandemic era to address challenges like student engagement and Zoom fatigue, underscoring the importance of student autonomy and flexibility. Overall, the paper presents significant insights into the effectiveness of the Interactive Synchronous HyFlex Model in maintaining student engagement and community perceptions in a blended learning environment during and after the COVID-19 pandemic.

STUDY 3: MENTZER, NATHAN, AND LAKSHMY MOHANDAS. 2022. "STUDENT EXPERIENCES IN AN INTERACTIVE SYNCHRONOUS HYFLEX DESIGN THINKING COURSE DURING COVID-19." *INTERACTIVE LEARNING ENVIRONMENTS* 32 (5): 1613–28.

QUICK LOOK	
PURPOSE	To understand how students experienced the Interactive Synchronous HyFlex model at the beginning of the COVID-19 pandemic.
KEY FINDINGS	Students appreciated the flexibility, sense of community, ease of communication, and preparation for future work environments offered by the HyFlex model. They also valued the accommodation of diverse learning preferences and the ability to continue participating when facing COVID-related disruptions. However, challenges included an initial software learning curve, difficulties for remote students in effectively navigating their environment, technological distractions, and variable motivation for remote participation.

RECOMMENDATIONS OR IMPLICATIONS	The study recommends more software training, clear expectations for remote participation, strategies to encourage camera use, addressing technology issues, and encouraging full engagement between face-to-face and remote students.
LINK	https://doi.org/10.1080/10494820.2022.2124423

The purpose of this Mentzer and Mohandas study was to understand how students experienced a blended synchronous learning approach that was gaining popularity due to COVID-19 during fall 2020. The research question that guided the study was: *How and in what ways did students experience the Interactive Synchronous HyFlex model at the start of the global pandemic in our active learning design course?*

Situated in the same course as the other studies reviewed in this paper, the study used a qualitative phenomenological method. Focus group interviews were conducted with students at the beginning, middle, and end of the semester. In total, eighty-four students participated across nineteen focus groups. Data were analyzed using inductive coding to identify key themes.

Results showed that students appreciated the affordances of the Interactive Synchronous HyFlex mode as an effective learning approach: providing flexibility in participation, fostering a sense of community, enabling ease of communication, and offering preparation for future jobs involving remote work. Additional benefits included accommodating different learning preferences, enabling continued participation when exposed to COVID, allowing comfortable interaction with instructors, and providing a collaborative environment.

Opportunities for improving the Interactive Synchronous HyFlex model were also identified. Students experienced an initial software learning curve when learning to use Microsoft Teams. Additionally, remote students did not always effectively navigate their environment. In some instances, remote students failed to speak up and gain the attention of their peers, placing more burden on their face-to-face peers. In other cases, remote students felt ignored by face-to-face group members. Additional challenges included technological distractions, audio echo/feedback problems, and variable motivation to engage in remote participation by both face-to-face and remote students.

These results underscore the necessity for providing more software training, setting clear expectations for remote participation and accountability, using strategies like requiring cameras, and monitoring engagement. Addressing technology issues and encouraging face-to-face students to fully engage with remote peers is also important. The study provides insights into student experiences with HyFlex learning that can inform implementation of blended synchronous approaches as the likely new normal in higher education post-pandemic.

STUDY 4: MENTZER, NATHAN, BHAWNA KRISHNA, ANKITA KOTANGALE, AND LAKSHMY MOHANDAS. 2023. "HYFLEX ENVIRONMENT: ADDRESSING STUDENTS' BASIC PSYCHOLOGICAL NEEDS." *LEARNING ENVIRONMENTS RESEARCH* 26 (1): 271–89.

QUICK LOOK	
PURPOSE	To quantitatively examine the extent to which the HyFlex model met students' basic psychological needs (BPN) compared to a traditional face-to-face-only environment.
KEY FINDINGS	The HyFlex environment demonstrated comparable or better satisfaction of autonomy, competence, and relatedness needs compared to the traditional face-to-face environment. Notably, frustration related to autonomy and competence was significantly lower in HyFlex. However, students participating remotely one or more times reported slightly or significantly lower satisfaction of some BPN compared to those consistently attending face-to-face.
RECOMMENDATIONS OR IMPLICATIONS	The study highlights an unexpected conflict: While HyFlex appears to meet students' BPN better than traditional environments overall, those who choose to participate remotely may experience slightly lower need satisfaction. This suggests a need for further investigation and potential adjustments to enhance the remote participation experience.
LINK	https://doi.org/10.1007/s10984-022-09431-z

In two previously described studies, students articulated experiences that indicated students' basic psychological needs (BPN) were being satisfied while participating in the Interactive Synchronous HyFlex model. However, as the nature of qualitative work is to understand and explain a phenomenon, we were curious about the extent to which this sense of psychological needs satisfaction was experienced by students in the course more broadly and how this might compare to students' experiences in the course prior to experiencing the HyFlex approach.

In response, this Mentzer et al. study launched a quantitative investigation examining the extent to which BPN were met before the pandemic in a traditional face-to-face-only version of the course compared to a version of the course using our HyFlex model.

This quasi-experimental study had two distinct components, each with its own research question and sample. First, we hypothesized that the HyFlex environment met students' BPN as well as or perhaps better than the traditional face-to-face-only environment. As a test for this hypothesis, we accessed BPN satisfaction data from fall 2019 and compared these to data collected during fall 2020 for a sample of 1,344 students. Data were collected as part of a university effort to maintain quality teaching and learning environments administered by the Center for Instructional Excellence using a validated and reliable survey called the Basic Psychological Needs Satisfaction and Frustration Scale (BPNSFS).

Independent samples t-tests indicated alignment with qualitative discoveries in the previous studies, further establishing that the HyFlex environment had comparable levels of autonomy satisfaction (the freedom to make decisions based on their interest in the course) and competence satisfaction (the capability to effectively fulfill what is required through classroom expectations) as well as relatedness to peers and instructors (connectedness among students when they collaboratively work together and have engaging interactions with their instructors). Interestingly, frustration associated with autonomy and competence was significantly lower in the HyFlex environment than the face-to-face-only environment.

The second component of this study narrowed the sample to focus on students in the HyFlex cohort during fall 2020 who had both attendance and BPNSFS data (n = 136) and was driven by the hypothesis that the BPN were met equally well for remote and face-to-face learners. Motivation for this question emerged from early qualitative data that suggested students appreciated the HyFlex environment although they may not have taken advantage of the opportunity to be remote. In addition, while students generally appreciated the autonomy and the safety net to participate remotely if needed, afforded by a HyFlex environment, they also recognized the additional complexities of blending face-to-face and remote members of their class and small group. Thus, we wondered if students who were remote at times felt the same sense of their BPN being met as those who engaged in the HyFlex environment but did not try remote participation.

A Mann-Whitney U test indicated that for five of the six measures of BPN, students in the HyFlex course who participated consistently through a face-to-face modality had slightly more positive results than students who participated once or more times remotely. The sense of relatedness to peers was significantly higher for students who chose to be face-to-face daily.

Results of this study provided an unexpected conflict: HyFlex meets students' BPN slightly or significantly better than face-to-face-only environments, but those students who take advantage of the HyFlex environment through participating remotely one or more days have slightly or significantly less satisfaction of their BPN.

STUDY 5: MENTZER, NATHAN J., TONYA M. ISABELL, AND LAKSHMY MOHANDAS. 2024. "THE IMPACT OF INTERACTIVE SYNCHRONOUS HYFLEX MODEL ON STUDENT ACADEMIC PERFORMANCE IN A LARGE ACTIVE LEARNING INTRODUCTORY COLLEGE DESIGN COURSE." *JOURNAL OF COMPUTING IN HIGHER EDUCATION* 36 (3): 619–46.

QUICK LOOK	
PURPOSE	To analyze the impact of the Interactive Synchronous HyFlex model on student academic performance, comparing grades between traditional face-to-face and HyFlex modalities, and between in-person and remote participants within HyFlex.
KEY FINDINGS	Students in HyFlex achieved significantly higher grades on the first project and showed significantly higher median ranks across all projects and final course grades compared to the traditional face-to-face modality. Within the HyFlex modality, in-person students had significantly higher median ranks on the second and third projects and final grades compared to those attending remotely one or more times.
RECOMMENDATIONS OR IMPLICATIONS	The study suggests that HyFlex can positively impact student academic performance. However, the differences between in-person and remote participants within HyFlex indicate a need to understand and address potential factors influencing the performance of remote learners.
LINK	https://doi.org/10.1007/s12528-023-09369-y

Our earlier studies concentrated on examining the impact of Interactive Synchronous HyFlex on students' BPN, but we knew little about how this instruction impacts students' academic performance. The experience of learning and collaborating with peers and instructors in HyFlex settings, initially designed for residential undergraduate students, was unusual and unexpected for students. Students needed to extensively use technology for communication, peer collaboration, and group projects. Due to the conflicting results of previous studies about the impact of HyFlex models on students' academic performance (He et al. 2015; Lakhal et al. 2014; Lightner and Lightner-Laws 2016; Miller et al. 2013; Rhoads 2020), we decided to analyze the impact of our Interactive Synchronous HyFlex model on academic performance. First, we compared the course grades between a traditional face-to-face-only modality course offering (fall 2019) and an Interactive Synchronous HyFlex course offering (fall 2020). Second, we focused on HyFlex instruction and analyzed whether the final course grades of students who exclusively chose to participate face-to-face differed from those who attended the class one or more times remotely.

This quantitative study included data from 1,344 students across two semesters: fall 2019 (traditional face-to-face-only mode) and fall 2020 (HyFlex modality). We had readily available attendance data on 483 students who participated in the HyFlex modality. As student grades are a widely accepted metric for evaluating student success (York et al. 2015), we gauged academic performance using student grades on three projects and final course grades. Before the analysis, we conducted a pre-analysis similarity check of students' Scholastic Assessment Test (SAT) scores and demographic data to determine the degree to which they were similar at the beginning of their academic terms.

To compare students' grades for the three projects and final course grades between traditional and HyFlex settings, we utilized a *t*-test and Mann-Whitney *U* test due to deviation from the normal distribution in the dependent variable. *T*-test results indicated that students received higher grades in HyFlex than in the traditional face-to-face-only learning environment for Project 1. The mean scores for the other projects and final course grades were similar between HyFlex and traditional face-to-face-only modalities. However, the Mann-Whitney *U* test results showed significantly higher mean rank scores for HyFlex in all projects and final course grades compared to the traditional face-to-face-only approach. To understand these conflicting results, we conducted a chi-square test, revealing that compared to traditional instruction, HyFlex students had a significantly different grade distribution, showing they received more A's and F's. Hence, the mean ranks were significantly different, while the mean scores were similar.

The second study narrowed the sample to only students in the HyFlex modality, comparing the academic performance of students who attended the class exclusively face-to-face and those students who chose to be remote one or more times. Our focus was on potential differences across three projects and final course grades. T-test results did not show significant differences between students who attended class face-to-face exclusively and those who participated one or more times remotely. Mann-Whitney U test results, however, indicated that face-to-face students significantly outperformed their one-or-more-times-remote counterparts in the second and third projects and final semester grades. Examining grade distribution closer revealed that face-to-face students received more A's and F's compared to their peers who attended one or more times remotely.

In conclusion, the results of both tests indicated that students' scores on the first project were significantly higher in the HyFlex modality. HyFlex's median ranks were significantly higher in all other grade measures (Project 2, Project 3, and final semester grades), whereas means were similar for the rest. Between face-to-face and one-or-more-times-remote students, t-tests and the Mann-Whitney U test indicated similar grades for Project 1. The median ranks were higher for face-to-face students, whereas the means in both modalities were similar in all other measures.

STUDY 6: MENTZER, NATHAN, SHAWN FARRINGTON, JENICA WOOLLEY, AND LAKSHMY MOHANDAS. 2025. "DEEP LEARNING." UNPUBLISHED WORK, CURRENTLY IN PROGRESS.

QUICK LOOK	
PURPOSE	To assess deep learning, measured by design performance documented in student design journals, in both traditional face-to-face and HyFlex settings.
KEY FINDINGS	Preliminary findings (as the study is ongoing) indicate no statistically significant differences in mean design performance scores between HyFlex and face-to-face modalities. However, HyFlex groups showed larger standard deviations, suggesting greater variability in performance levels.

RECOMMENDATIONS OR IMPLICATIONS	This study suggests that HyFlex can support deep learning comparable to traditional settings, but with a wider range of outcomes. Further research is needed to explore the factors contributing to this variability and to refine instructional strategies to enhance deep learning for all students in HyFlex environments.
LINK	N/A

While grades are a traditional measure of academic success and commonly used to determine university progression, they not may be reflective of effort and/or performance (Banta et al. 1996). Understanding students' learning allows educators to assess the effectiveness of instructional strategies, digital tools, and learning resources in promoting meaningful engagement and the development of higher-order cognitive skills.

Currently a work in progress, this study uses a quasi-experimental design, considering a random sample of seventy-two design journals from teams from the design thinking course. Using a design journal rubric developed by Abts (Groves et al. 2014), researchers compared team design journals from spring and fall 2019 (face-to-face traditional group) to team design journals from fall 2021 and spring 2022 (HyFlex treatment group). Specifically, the rubric measures thirteen dimensions of design thinking, from problem identification to idea generation and evaluation and prototyping to testing and reflection on solution performance.

First, two researchers piloted the design rubric by independently rating twelve design journals. Next, the researchers compared their work, negotiating consensus during a few iterative sessions in order to establish a 90% inter-rater reliability measure spanning twenty design journals. Finally, in the time available for this project, one researcher was able to evaluate seventy-two journals randomly selected from fall and spring 2019, when the course was offered as face-to-face-only and fall 2021 and spring 2022, when the course was offered as HyFlex.

Results of the comparison offered two insights. First, independent samples t-tests indicated that the means were not significantly different across course modalities, with scores from the HyFlex offering at 28.40, whereas face-to-face-only offering was 28.65, which was marginally higher and neither practically nor statistically different. In addition, the standard deviation of the scores was larger for the HyFlex groups, which coincides with our previous studies indicating that grade distributions in HyFlex were wider such that some students and teams were more successful, while others were less successful.

STUDY 7: MOHANDAS, LAKSHMY, NATHAN MENTZER, ADRIE KOEHLER, SHAWN FARRINGTON, AND ELNARA MAMMADOVA. 2023. "UNDERSTANDING STUDENTS' SELF-REGULATION IN A HYFLEX DESIGN THINKING COURSE." IN *2023 ASEE ANNUAL CONFERENCE & EXPOSITION*. ASEE.

QUICK LOOK	
PURPOSE	To investigate the relationship between students' self-regulation skills and their daily participation choices (absent, remote, or face-to-face) in a HyFlex class.
KEY FINDINGS	Higher face-to-face participation was associated with lower self-regulated control of learning beliefs. However, no significant correlations were found between participation mode and critical thinking, metacognitive self-regulation, effort regulation, or peer learning.
RECOMMENDATIONS OR IMPLICATIONS	The findings suggest that while students may generally adapt their self-regulation strategies effectively across modalities, those who choose more face-to-face participation may perceive a lower need for self-regulated control of learning. This could point to subtle differences in the learning experiences and challenges associated with each modality.
LINK	https://peer.asee.org/understanding-students-self-regulation-in-a-hyflex-design-thinking-course.pdf

HyFlex learning models have grown in popularity since the onset of the COVID-19 pandemic (Calafiore and Giudici 2021; Padilla Rodriguez 2022), and research has shown promising academic outcomes for higher education contexts using HyFlex (Penrod 2022). Additionally, research suggests that student self-regulation impacts academic outcomes in traditional face-to-face learning environments (Kashif and Shahid 2021). However, less is known regarding student self-regulation in HyFlex instructional modalities in higher education.

This study explored the relationship between students' self-regulation and their daily participation choices (absent, remote, or face-to-face). Strong self-regulation skills can benefit students as they navigate HyFlex participation modalities, especially when the course context is problem-centered and requires significant small group interaction. For instance, Mentzer and Mohandas (2022) shared that the engagement level of some remote attendees is lower in their HyFlex learning format. As such, we hypothesized that students need higher levels of self-regulation when attending remotely in order to be successful. We used the following research question for the study: *What is the relationship between students' self-regulation and their choice of daily participation in a HyFlex class?*

This quantitative study took place in the spring 2022 semester considering seventeen course sections. We employed the Motivated Strategies for Learning Questionnaire (MSLQ) to determine the relationship between students' self-regulation and their participation choice in the HyFlex instructional format. The MSLQ is a widely cited survey instrument composed of more than fifteen scales that contains two sections: motivation and learning strategies. As a modularly designed instrument, each scale can be used independently (Pintrich 1991). As such, five scales, ranging from 1 to 7, were selected because they were the most appropriate for the study context: control of learning beliefs (α = 0.68), critical thinking (α = 0.80), metacognitive self-regulation (α = 0.79), effort regulation (α = 0.69), and peer learning (α = 0.76). The five scales were combined into one questionnaire and shared with 579 students as part of a larger survey administered at the conclusion of the semester. This resulted in a total of 331 respondents. Additionally, attendance data were collected from all of the course instructors for the entire semester. The course had twenty-nine meetings, and instructors kept records whether students joined face-to-face (F2F), remotely, or were absent.

To calculate a correlation between attendance choice and self-regulation, a ratio of modality was calculated as a percentage of F2F participation by dividing the number of F2F meetings attended by the total number of meetings in which the student participated, either F2F or remotely. Absences were not considered in the computation, because the emphasis was placed on students' daily decisions regarding their preferred mode of participation (remote or face-to-face). This is especially relevant since the course was originally conducted in a face-to-face format, and HyFlex was introduced to ensure continued participation during the pandemic. In a case where a student attended twenty-four meetings face-to-face, participated remotely in three meetings, and was absent for two meetings, the student's face-to-face percentage would be calculated as 24/(24 + 3), resulting in 88.9%. Subsequently, Pearson correlations were computed using the percentage of face-to-face attendance and each of the five relevant components/subcomponents of self-regulation.

On average, students strongly believed in their ability to control learning (mean score: 5.47). The Pearson correlation (r = −0.15, p = 0.005) revealed that higher face-to-face participation was associated with lower self-regulated control of learning belief. Students perceived a mean critical thinking score of 5.09, indicating a belief in applying previous knowledge in their HyFlex class. The nonsignificant Pearson correlation ($r = -0.103$, $p = 0.061$) showed that the mode of participation (face-to-face or remote) was not significantly correlated with students' critical thinking. Metacognitive self-regulation scored 4.70, indicating a moderate belief in applying awareness, knowledge, and control of cognition in their HyFlex class. The nonsignificant Pearson correlation ($r = -0.083$, $p = 0.134$) showed that students who chose face-to-face or remote participation had a comparable experience in applying cognitive skills. Effort regulation scored 4.86, signifying a moderate belief in their ability to control effort and attention in their HyFlex class. The nonsignificant Pearson correlation ($r = 0.019$, $p = 0.773$) indicated that students who opted for face-to-face or remote participation had a comparable experience in effort regulation. Students, on average, scored 4.58 in peer learning, indicating a moderate belief in working and learning with peers in their HyFlex class. The nonsignificant Pearson correlation ($r = -0.020$, $p = 0.716$) revealed that face-to-face and remote participants had similar experiences in peer learning.

STUDY 8: KRISHNA, BHAWNA. 2023. "EFFECT OF MODALITIES ON GROUP PERFORMANCE IN HYFLEX ENVIRONMENT." MASTER'S THESIS, PURDUE UNIVERSITY.

QUICK LOOK	
PURPOSE	To understand the academic success of teams in HyFlex environments, considering the impact of blending remote and face-to-face members on group performance.
KEY FINDINGS	The study found a slight negative correlation between the extent of remote participation within a team and students' grades on group projects.
RECOMMENDATIONS OR IMPLICATIONS	The findings suggest that while HyFlex allows for remote participation and can maintain or slightly improve overall grades, teams with more remote members tend to perform slightly less well. This reinforces the importance of in-person interaction for teamwork and suggests a need to develop strategies to enhance collaboration in hybrid teams.
LINK	https://doi.org/10.25394/PGS.23744424.v1

As we began to realize that the impact of participating in a HyFlex course was not the same for all students, we recognized that our analysis had been focusing on individual students' experiences in the course, although much of the coursework was in team-based experiences. This thesis study offered a unique contribution because the analysis was conducted at the group level rather than the individual level, accounting for students' immediate interactions with their peers.

To better understand the academic success of teams as they blend remote and face-to-face members, we analyzed grades from two larger group projects: Project 2 and Project 3. Project 2 spanned approximately four weeks with team members from similar majors assigned by the instructor. The learning goal of this project was to contextualize design thinking work within students' majors. Project 3 was the final course project and spanned approximately eight weeks. Teams were self-selected and situated in grand global challenges such as clean water, alternative energies, and urban infrastructure. For this project student teams identify a local opportunity to work on a problem that has global significance.

This study included 645 students enrolled in the course during fall 2021. For Project 2 students formed 168 groups, and for Project 3 there were 146 groups. Group assignments were graded by section instructors or graduate students dedicated to grading. All assignments had rubrics and instructions that had been refined each semester for clarity, validity, and reliability. Grading was led by two course coordinators who provided explanation, practice, support, and monitoring to ensure calibration and consistency. Attendance data were kept for students by class instructors.

A correlation analysis was used to inspect potential relationships between the extent to which teams of students participated remotely and their grades. Two variables were created for analysis for each project to test for correlation. First, "Group Remoteness" was computed for each team. For example, a team of four students who met for Project 2 during six class meetings had a total of twenty-four potential attendance measures. The number of meetings each team member was remote were counted and a ratio was computed. In this example, a team that had one student remote four times and another student remote twice had a total of six remote attendances of twenty-four possible, which was a ratio of 6/24, or 25% remote participation. Second, group grades for the project were calculated by averaging the grades received across students in the group. Group grades for Project 2 were typically the same for all students in the group unless they were absent, while grades for Project 3 were modified using a measure of contribution calculated for each student with input from peers.

Results indicated a slight negative correlation between the extent to which the team engaged with each other remotely and their grades for both projects. These findings indicated that at a team level, the extent to which one or more members contributed remotely is unrelated (or only very slightly related) to their modality. These results align with findings from the individual level in our previous study and reinforce the message that, when possible, students should be face-to-face, because we hypothesize that communication and teamwork are easier when all students in the team are together. These results also align with the findings from our previous study that suggest grades are similar or slightly higher in the HyFlex environment because students who might otherwise be absent and nonparticipating have an option to contribute to the group effort remotely and synchronously.

STUDY 9: MENTZER, NATHAN, ELNARA MAMMADOVA, ADRIE KOEHLER, LAKSHMY MOHANDAS, AND SHAWN FARRINGTON. 2025. "ANALYZING THE IMPACT OF BASIC PSYCHOLOGICAL NEEDS ON STUDENT ACADEMIC PERFORMANCE: A COMPARISON OF POST-PANDEMIC INTERACTIVE SYNCHRONOUS HYFLEX AND PRE-PANDEMIC TRADITIONAL FACE-TO-FACE INSTRUCTION." *EDUCATIONAL TECHNOLOGY RESEARCH AND DEVELOPMENT* 73 (1): 91–114.

QUICK LOOK	
PURPOSE	To examine the impact of Interactive Synchronous HyFlex on students' basic psychological needs (BPN) and academic performance in the post-pandemic era compared to the traditional face-to-face-only mode used pre-COVID-19.
KEY FINDINGS	HyFlex significantly enhanced students' BPN (autonomy, competence, relatedness to instructor and peers) in the post-pandemic era compared to the traditional mode. Key predictors of academic performance differed between the two modes. In traditional teaching, competence satisfaction, relatedness to peers, gender, and semester term were significant predictors, while in HyFlex, relatedness to the instructor, gender, and class rank were the leading predictors.

RECOMMENDATIONS OR IMPLICATIONS	The study highlights the sustained benefits of HyFlex for students' psychological needs beyond the immediate context of the pandemic. The differences in predictors of academic performance between the two modes underscore the need for tailored instructional strategies to support student success in HyFlex environments.
LINK	https://doi.org/10.1007/s11423-024-10417-2

Although our HyFlex model developed as a response to the pandemic, we continued teaching in this mode when the disruptive impact of the pandemic was minimal. In early 2023, the COVID-19 pandemic was declared a nonemergency internationally (World Health Organization 2023). Therefore, we decided to analyze the feasibility of Interactive Synchronous HyFlex for the post-pandemic era. This quantitative study examined the impact of the Interactive Synchronous HyFlex mode from two perspectives. First, we considered how the Interactive Synchronous HyFlex course design addresses students' fundamental psychological needs in the post-pandemic era, differing from the traditional face-to-face-only course delivery method utilized pre-COVID-19. Second, we examined the impact of BPN and demographic factors on students' academic performance in the Interactive Synchronous HyFlex and traditional course delivery modes.

The study considered students' final course grades (n = 2,558), the BPN survey results (n = 1,203), SAT scores, and demographic information. Demographics affirmed that most students were in their first or second year by credit hour. Students represented nine groups of diverse ethnicities, including White, Asian American, Hispanic/Latino, two or more races, Black or African American, Native Hawaiian or Other Pacific Islander, and American Indian or Alaska Native. About 11% of students were international and classified by the university as "international" regardless of their ethnicity.

We used data from four semesters, fall 2019/2022 and spring 2020/2023, because fall and spring tend to yield different student experiences. The course was taught traditionally (face-to-face-only participation) in spring and fall 2019, which occurred before the pandemic era. In fall 2022 and spring 2023, the treatment semesters, the course was delivered using HyFlex instruction. Given that the primary course audience was first-year students, who typically enroll in the fall semester (while upper-level students who have not yet taken the course tend to enroll in the spring term), we anticipated and statistically accounted for differences between the fall and spring semesters. SAT scores served as a proxy pretest to ensure academic comparability among students before analysis, and demographic variables were incorporated to confirm uniformity across demographic characteristics.

To examine the impact of Interactive Synchronous HyFlex on students' BPN in the post-pandemic era compared to traditional face-to-face-only teaching, we utilized independent sample t-tests. Results were slightly different for the fall and spring semesters. In the spring semesters, all four BPN scores (autonomy satisfaction, competence satisfaction, relatedness to instructor, and relatedness to peer) were significantly higher for the Interactive Synchronous HyFlex mode than the traditional mode. The effect sizes of the differences indicated minimal, small, and medium effects, as *Cohen's d* ranged from 0.187 to 0.519 (Cohen 1992). In the fall semesters, however, only three BPN scores (autonomy satisfaction, relatedness to instructor, and relatedness to peer) were significantly higher for the HyFlex model; the exception, competence satisfaction, was only marginally higher. The effect sizes of differences indicated small and medium, as *Cohen's d* ranged from 0.247 to 0.553. These results differ from our Study 3 (Mentzer and Mohandas 2022), which compared the pre-pandemic traditional mode to HyFlex during the pandemic. In that study, we did not find a significant difference in BPN satisfaction scores, and effect sizes were very small, as *Cohen's d* ranged from 0.01 to 0.13.

After analyzing the impact of the Interactive Synchronous HyFlex model on BPN scores in pre-pandemic time, we investigated which of the BPN indicators are a significant predictor of students' academic achievement in both teaching modes alongside demographic variables and semester. A multiple regression analysis was completed. As a subcategory of demographic variables, gender was coded as a binary variable: "female" and "male." Class rank was classified into three categories based on credit hours students had before enrolling on the course: "0–29 credit hours," "30–59 credit hours," and "60+ credit hours." As the residency variable, we had two categories: "domestic" and "foreign." The ethnicity had four categories: "underrepresented," "overrepresented," "international," and "unknown." However, as the university automatically considered students as international who indicated their residency as foreign, it led to a multicollinearity issue within the dataset. Hence, we removed international from the ethnicity category to ensure robustness of the results. We grouped semesters into two categories since we ran two separate regression analyses for HyFlex and traditional modes. Each group had fall and spring semesters represented with separate dummy variables to let us capture variations in final course grades across semesters.

Results showed that all variables (BPN, gender, class rank, ethnicity, semester) could significantly predict students' final course grades in both traditional teaching $[F(11, 758) = 5.54, p = < 0.001, \text{with } R^2 = 0.061]$ and in Interactive Synchronous HyFlex $[F(11, 421) = 5.01, p < 0.001, \text{with } R^2 = 0.093]$ modes. Among BPN scores, competence satisfaction ($B = 1.35, \beta = 0.18, p < 0.001$) and relatedness to peers ($B = 1.104, \beta = 0.127, p = 0.002$) were significant predictors of students' final grades in traditional teaching. However, in the HyFlex mode, only relatedness to instructor ($B = 0.739, \beta = 0.132, p = 0.045$) was a significant predictor.

Among demographic variables, gender was a significant predictor of final course grades both in traditional ($B = 2.625, \beta = 0.144, p < 0.001$) and in HyFlex modes ($B = 3.164, \beta = 0.195, p < 0.001$) because female students tend to get higher grades than their male counterparts. The other demographic variables (ethnicity, class rank, and residency) were not significant predictors in the traditional mode. However, in HyFlex, ethnicity and class rank were significant predictors. In the ethnicity category, compared to the overrepresented peers (reference group), students with "unknown" ethnicity received statistically significantly higher grades ($B = 4.027, \beta = 0.075, p < 0.001$). In class rank, the 30–59 credit hours group was associated with a statistically significant increase in a final course grade ($B = 1.664, \beta = 0.11, p = 0.027$). Regarding semesters, it was a significant predictor of final grades only in traditional teaching and learning mode because students tended to get significantly lower grades in the spring of 2019 ($B = -1.458, \beta = -0.09, p = 0.017$) compared to the fall of 2019 (reference group).

In summary, findings indicated that, post-pandemic, the Interactive Synchronous HyFlex course design significantly enhanced students' BPN compared to the traditional pre-pandemic mode. The key predictors of academic performance in traditional face-to-face teaching included competence satisfaction, relatedness to peers, gender, and semester term. In contrast, in the Interactive Synchronous HyFlex model, the leading predictive factors were relatedness to the instructor, gender, and class rank. The result about the predictiveness of relatedness to the instructor in academic performance led us to investigate how Interactive Synchronous HyFlex fostered a connection between students and instructors to increase their academic performance.

STUDY 10: KOEHLER, ADRIE, LAKSHMY MOHANDAS, NATHAN MENTZER, AND ELNARA MAMMADOVA. 2025. "TEACHING ACROSS MODALITIES: HYFLEX INSTRUCTOR PRESENCE." MANUSCRIPT UNDER REVIEW.

QUICK LOOK	
PURPOSE	To investigate how instructor presence is established in HyFlex classrooms and whether variations in instructor approaches are associated with student perceptions of instructor presence
KEY FINDINGS	Three instructors demonstrated distinct approaches to establishing presence in HyFlex, differing in their use of technology, attendance requirements, and emphasis on student autonomy. However, despite these differences, student perceptions of instructor presence remained consistently positive across the three sections.
RECOMMENDATIONS OR IMPLICATIONS	The study highlights the flexibility instructors have in establishing presence in HyFlex, suggesting that various approaches can lead to positive student experiences. Further research could explore the specific elements of instructor presence most impactful for student learning and engagement in hybrid settings.
LINK	N/A

As much of our previous work focused on the student experience, we were curious about how instructors were specifically facilitating HyFlex learning experiences and whether there were differences in how HyFlex facilitation impacted students. Specifically, we investigated how instructor presence is established in HyFlex classrooms and whether variance in instructor approaches is associated with how students perceive instructor presence.

In this case study–mixed methods approach, we used the CoI framework to capture how three instructors established instructor presence in their courses. We used Richardson et al.'s (2015) definition of instructor presence: "the specific actions and behaviors taken by the instructor that projects him/herself as a real person . . . [and] is more likely to be manifested in the 'live' part of courses—as they are being implemented—as opposed to during the course design process." Each instructor represented a single case. Our data sources included instructor interviews, instructor observations, and student responses to the CoI survey. We first created a profile for each instructor's presence by investigating their reasoning for adopting specific approaches and considering their students' perceptions of their presence. Next, we compared across cases to identify similarities and differences.

We had convenient access to a full dataset for three instructors and their students. Specifically, we used semi-structured interviews with instructors, asking questions aligned with the CoI framework to determine how they believed they were establishing presence in a HyFlex environment and their motives for facilitating HyFlex learning in the way that they did. Next, we analyzed recorded course sessions for each instructor to identify specific examples of instructor presence. Finally, students from each instructor's section were asked to complete the CoI survey. Using a one-way ANOVA, we compared students' responses across the three sections.

The three instructors, Ben, Lia, and Tom (pseudonyms used to protect identity), used specific strategies when creating instructor presence in HyFlex:

> Ben valued HyFlex, focused on promoting its relevance as a professional tool students would use in their future, used a variety of technologies to establish and extend his presence, required all students to join the class via Microsoft Teams meetings each session, and was very available to his students practically at all times. His students indicated positive perceptions of his presence.
>
> Lia saw Hyflex as a short-term temporary solution, used a variety of technologies to establish and maintain presence, checked with face-to-face and remote students frequently, and required all students to join the class Teams meetings each session. Her students indicated positive perceptions of her presence.
>
> Tom downplayed HyFlex, emphasized that remote attendance be used sparingly, provided specific reasons for when HyFlex could be used, required only remote students and teams with remote students to log into Teams meetings, and offered remote students alternative ways of participating in class through using technologies. His students indicated positive perceptions of his presence.

Across the three cases, instructors regularly monitored remote student participation, checked-in with students, supported team collaboration, and used technologies to extend presence. However, requirements for joining Teams, the use of the chat tool, how technologies were implemented to support multimodalities, and instructor availability beyond class time varied. The results of the one-way ANOVA revealed no significant differences across sections, suggesting that regardless of key qualitative (from observation and interview data) differences in instructor presence, students' perceptions remained consistently positive.

Key takeaways from this research include (1) instructors can establish and maintain presence in HyFlex classrooms in different ways; (2) instructors revealed a range in their beliefs and use of technology, attendance, and student autonomy; and (3) different instructor presence can lead to positive student experiences. Regardless of clear differences in how instructors established their presence, students appeared to follow and accept whatever norms were created. This research offers deeper understanding of the facilitation of HyFlex learning environments and how instructor presence is established.

STUDY 11: MAMMADOVA, ELNARA, NATHAN MENTZER, LAKSHMY MOHANDAS AND ADRIE KOEHLER. 2025. "ONBOARDING TO HYFLEX AS A NEW INSTRUCTOR." UNPUBLISHED WORK, CURRENTLY IN PROGRESS.

QUICK LOOK	
PURPOSE	To explore the lived experiences of two new instructors as they implement the Interactive Synchronous HyFlex model in their classrooms in a post-pandemic learning environment.
KEY FINDINGS	Three key themes emerged: communication, technical operations, and the learning curve. Challenges included establishing clear communication with students about HyFlex expectations, navigating new software and hardware, and managing the learning curve for both instructors and students.
RECOMMENDATIONS OR IMPLICATIONS	The results suggested several strategies for improving the onboarding experience for new HyFlex instructors, including embedding links to remote platforms in the learning management system, clarifying student and instructor roles and responsibilities, providing opportunities for instructors to practice with technology, and creating assignments that familiarize students with hybrid collaboration.
LINK	N/A

As Interactive Synchronous HyFlex implementation has been refined and the impact on students has generally been positive in terms of student experience,

BPN, grades, and learning, in this research we emphasize the experience of becoming a HyFlex instructor. This study, currently in the analysis phase, is qualitative and seeks to understand the lived experiences of two new instructors in the post-pandemic learning environment as they implement Interactive Synchronous HyFlex.

In fall 2023, the instructional team had two new instructors. These two instructors agreed to engage in a collaborative autoethnography with an experienced instructor, who is the lead researcher on the HyFlex research grant. Following a method described by McDonald et al. (2022), each week, the two new instructors journaled and met for thirty to forty-five minutes to collaboratively reflect on their experiences. Both instructors, who were starting MS degrees in STEM education, previously had educational experiences preparing them to be instructors in HyFlex learning environments (one was a teaching assistant in a blended course; the other a former STEM middle school teacher during COVID).

Each week, the instructors responded to prompts about how they prepared for their HyFlex courses, how their courses went, and potential opportunities for improvement. The lead instructor reviewed these reflections prior to facilitating a discussion with the two new instructors at the end of each week and served as both a facilitator of the focus group interviews and a participant engaging in discussion, resulting in feedback based on experience and previous research findings. Thus, the instructors' questions and concerns often led to ideas that were implemented and discussed at future meetings for additional reflection. Using discussion and reflection data, the lead researcher identified emergent themes, reaching consensus with the other instructors through additional discussion.

Three themes emerged from the discussion: communication, technical operations, and a learning curve. As an emergent theme, communication with students was critical—both what needed to be communicated and how the message was communicated to students. Initial university-level communication indicated the course would be offered in a face-to-face modality; however, the syllabus indicated students could participate temporarily remotely as needed. Therefore, instructors had to define "temporary" and when remote participation was reasonable, share expectations about blending face-to-face and remote participation, describe how to access the general channel and team channels, and track remote attendance in real time to support team collaboration.

Technical hardware and software operation was another emergent theme for both the instructors and students. Microsoft Teams was generally new to students and was new to both instructors, and navigating the complexities of the new software was a challenge. Particularly, students struggled with transitioning from one Teams channel to another, which was complicated by the instructors' difficulties supporting students in this process due to their limited experience. Additionally, the instructors shared that they experienced technical problems in interfacing across hardware as they managed large monitors, personal laptops, external microphones, and speakers while simultaneously navigating the system to coordinate these devices.

The instructors discussed the learning curve for both them and their students. While the learning curve is inherently related to the other themes (communication and technical operation), we saw it as a separate consideration. Before the start of the semester, the instructors completed an orientation on HyFlex and were given a document outlining conceptual, technical, and procedural aspects of HyFlex. Despite these preparation efforts, they had difficulties the first weeks of the semester when facilitating HyFlex learning for forty students with unfamiliar hardware and software (e.g., playing video in class, handling unexpected software updates, handling Windows versus Apple OS). Furthermore, while procedures for students initially seemed clear, the instructors shared that since the course is primarily set up as a face-to-face learning environment, where remote participation is temporary, most students who were remote were doing it for the first or second time. Therefore, the remote students were unfamiliar with the process and needed support every time class met throughout the term.

As an ongoing study, we anticipate key implications related to communication and technical aspects easing the learning curve by driving changes in future implementations. Regarding communication, in addition to scheduling meetings using Microsoft products (Outlook and Teams), we suggest embedding a link to the general Microsoft Teams channel (where each class starts) in the course learning management system (LMS), such that students who are remote and have not installed the Outlook and/or Teams applications on their devices will have additional access points. Additionally, roles and responsibilities must be considered deliberately. Remote learners should log into the LMS and to Microsoft Teams before the start of class and look for the meeting and content. When students are remote, they should communicate with their small groups to remind everyone that they will be joining remotely. Face-to-face students will have a similar routine where they reach out to a missing student to establish communication and connect with them synchronously in the team channel. On the technical side for instructors, instructional leaders can create a list of technical challenges to be anticipated, and much like a driver education test, we can challenge new instructors to navigate these situations ahead of the semester. In addition to watching an experienced HyFlex instructor, new instructors could be challenged to demonstrate competency on their hardware with their operating system and current set of updates. For students, an assignment early in the term where they launch a meeting in their team channel to blend remote and face-to-face learners may increase familiarity so that when it is needed, they are ready rather than figuring it out on the fly by themselves.

STUDY 12: MAMMADOVA, ELNARA, NATHAN MENTZER, AND EMRE TOPALGOKCELI. 2025. "IMPACT OF DISABILITY ACCOMMODATIONS ON LEARNING EXPERIENCES AMONG UNDERGRADUATE STUDENTS IN HYFLEX." PAPER PRESENTED AT THE AMERICAN EDUCATIONAL RESEARCH ASSOCIATION ANNUAL MEETING, DENVER, CO, APRIL.

QUICK LOOK	
PURPOSE	To determine whether HyFlex instruction enhances the learning and performance of students with disabilities compared to those without accommodations.
KEY FINDINGS	Preliminary findings indicate that the learning experiences of students with and without accommodations were not equivalent in terms of academic performance and basic psychological needs. Students with accommodations had higher mean grades but reported lower satisfaction of BPN. Sentiment analysis revealed that the level of positive feedback was higher than the level of negative feedback for both groups. Students with accommodations reported higher positive sentiments in autonomy satisfaction compared to students without accommodation. However, this trend was reversed for engagement.
RECOMMENDATIONS OR IMPLICATIONS	The study highlights the need for tailored approaches within HyFlex to address the unique needs of students with disabilities. While the flexibility of HyFlex may benefit these students, further research is needed to understand the nuances of their experiences and to ensure equitable outcomes.
LINK	N/A

In our previous studies, we examined the impact of Interactive Synchronous HyFlex instruction on overall student performance. This study focuses specifically on determining whether HyFlex instruction enhances the learning and performance of students with disabilities. While some literature uses "disabled person" and "person with disability" interchangeably, this study intentionally employs person-first language, such as "students with disabilities," to emphasize the individual rather than the disability. This linguistic approach underscores the humanity and multidimensional nature of each person, recognizing disability as just one part of their identity (Crocker and Smith 2019). Research shows that the underrepresentation of students with disabilities (SwD) in science, technology, engineering, and mathematics (STEM) majors in higher education remains a significant issue (Love et al. 2015; Pfeifer et al. 2020). Moreover, our literature review did not show any research on the experiences of students with disabilities in HyFlex classrooms. This study investigated the learning experiences of undergraduate students who officially requested accommodation from the Disability Resource Center in an introductory human-centered design course that was delivered through Interactive Synchronous HyFlex instruction.

This study utilized secondary data from 3,777 undergraduate students enrolled in an introductory human-centered design course between fall 2021 and spring 2024, which was implemented using an Interactive Synchronous HyFlex instruction approach. Under the Americans with Disabilities Act (ADA) and Section 504 of the Rehabilitation Act of 1973, students who requested accommodation through the Disability Resource Center at the university are defined as students with disabilities. However, not every student with disabilities registers at the disability office or requests accommodation through that office (Schelly et al. 2011; Wagner et al. 2005) This fact prevents us from defining students who did not ask for accommodation as students without disabilities. To avoid this misrepresentation, in this study we defined them as students with accommodation (SwA) and without accommodation (SwoA). In total, 127 participants (3.4%) requested accommodation. We used students' final course grade, BPN survey results, and answers to open-ended questions on BPN. The usable data for analysis included a total of 1,582 responses from 768 (30 SwA and 738 SwoA) participants.

We addressed our research questions in two steps of analysis: test of equivalency and sentiment analysis. The test of equivalency was used to analyze whether final course grades and BPN were similar enough to say that accommodative HyFlex instruction did not make a practical difference between the group of SwA and SwoA. Unlike traditional tests of differences, equivalency specifically tests whether the group differences are small enough to be considered practically insignificant within prespecified boundaries (Lakens et al. 2018). The equivalence bounds were set based on raw scores at ±0.26 for final course grade, ±0.46 for autonomy satisfaction, ±0.32 for competence satisfaction, ±0.41 for relatedness to instructor, and ±0.43 for relatedness to peers (Lakens et al. 2018). Differences smaller than these bounds were considered negligible. All two one-sided tests (TOST) results were nonsignificant, indicating that experiences of SwA and SwoA were not equivalent in academic performance, $t(135.4) = -0.00, p = 0.50$; autonomy satisfaction, $t(48.65) = -0.00, p = 0.50$; competence satisfaction, $t(48.26) = -0.00, p = 0.50$; relatedness to instructor, $t(48.19) = -0.00, p = 0.50$; and relatedness to peer, $t(48.11) = -0.00, p = 0.50$. Thus, these results indicated that mean scores of SwA were higher for the grade variable but lower for the satisfaction of BPN.

To explore the nuances of nonequivalence between SwA and SwoA, we employed a natural language processing (NLP) technique. We conducted sentiment analysis on students' open-ended responses from the BPN-related survey to capture their opinions and sentiments (Birjali et al. 2021; Liu 2022). Given the nature of the student data, to determine the best library we randomly sampled 334 of the 1,582 responses (Israel 1992) and manually assessed their positive and negative sentiments. This sample was then validated against forty-three NLP models. We recorded the accuracy and F1 scores of each model in aligning with our manual sentiment analysis. The Roberta Large English library with the highest F1 score, at 92%, was selected for our sentiment analysis. The results indicated that SwA provided highly positive feedback on autonomy satisfaction (100%), followed by relatedness to the instructor (92.8%) and competence satisfaction (85.7%). The SwA group used the least positive words in engagement, with a 75% positive rate. The SwoA group expressed the most positive feedback on relatedness to the instructor (89.1%), followed by autonomy satisfaction (88.4%) and engagement (86.5%). The least satisfactory feedback from this group was related to competence satisfaction, with a 17.2% negative rate.

Our preliminary findings suggested that two groups of students had distinct learning experiences in academic performance and BPN in the HyFlex environment and these differences are not small enough to be deemed negligible. Based on their mean scores, we can conclude that SwA did better than their SwoA counterparts, except for BPN. These differences highlight the necessity for tailored approaches within the HyFlex model to address the unique needs of SwA, ensuring that they receive adequate support to achieve similar outcomes as SwoA.

Further exploration through sentiment analysis revealed that Interactive Synchronous HyFlex instruction supports strong connections between students and instructors, particularly for SwA. This group reported highly positive feedback (100%) regarding autonomy satisfaction, indicating that the flexibility of the HyFlex model was particularly beneficial for them. However, the relatively higher negative feedback on engagement points to an area needing attention, particularly for SwA (25%). The results of the sentiment analysis on BPN necessitate further research to understand why SwA reported lower BPN scores yet expressed more positive feedback on their satisfaction levels.

SUMMARY OF THE ARTICLES

The summaries from eleven studies highlight the efficacy of Interactive Synchronous HyFlex settings as a supporting system of students' learning and BPN, often either similar or better than traditional face-to-face settings. For instance, Study 5 reported significantly higher student grades in HyFlex classrooms for the first course project and significantly higher median ranks for the rest of the course projects and students' final course grades, showcasing the adaptability of the Interactive Synchronous HyFlex approach and adding to a growing body of HyFlex literature (Calafiore and Giudici 2021; He et al. 2015; Lakhal et al. 2014; Magana et al. 2022; Miller et al. 2013; Rhoads 2020). Study 9 revealed that the HyFlex environment meets students' BPN significantly better, not only during the COVID-19 pandemic, as Study 4 stated, but also after the pandemic era, which builds on two related studies by Bozan et al. (2024) and Holzer et al. (2021). Additionally, HyFlex created an effective environment for robust facilitation of team learning compared to face-to-face instruction by allowing students to be part of the team remotely and synchronously whenever needed (Study 8). This option was highly supported by students in Study 3, which is evidence of students' strong self-regulation skills over controlling learning that emphasizes students' adaptability to different learning modalities.

EXPECTATIONS AND MESSAGING

Several of our studies highlight recommendations for improving teaching and learning experiences in HyFlex, including clear communication between students and instructors and sharing well-defined expectations about attendance modality with students, which have been a theme in existing literature (Howell 2022; Kohnke and Moorhouse 2021; Rasheed et al. 2020). Study 4 reported that students who joined the class remotely one or more times were less satisfied, considering their BPN. Study 5 reported that the mean ranks of grades for students who joined lessons face-to-face and one or more times remotely were similar throughout their three course projects, but the median ranks were higher for face-to-face students. Nevertheless, whether students joined lessons remotely or face-to-face, they had similar experiences in terms of effort regulation, applying cognitive skills, and peer learning (Study 7); their choice of class participation did not affect their sense of classroom community (Study 2), but their teamwork and communication might be easier if students were face-to-face (Study 8). These results indicate that instructors need to clearly communicate expectations and definitions of attendance, ensuring that students comprehend engagement parameters. The need for clear communication of expectations for participation modality and its accountability was also reinforced by the new instructors in Study 11. These insights illustrate the importance of instructional design that bridges the gap between face-to-face and remote participation, fostering an inclusive and effective learning community.

COURSE DESIGN AND FACILITATION

The findings of our studies highlight the pivotal role of coordinated design across multiple layers in HyFlex learning environments, while building on previous work by Miller et al. (2013). As revealed in Studies 1 and 3, considerations of the availability of technology for the institution, instructors, and students, along with the physical classroom setup, emerged as crucial factors influencing the success of HyFlex implementation. Additionally, establishing upfront values such as keeping cameras on for social presence and fruitful team collaboration, using headsets to improve audio experience and reduce potential disruptions in a hybrid environment, and continuing to monitor student interaction through Microsoft Teams channels serves as a foundational layer, impacting the overall effectiveness and engagement levels within HyFlex structures (Mentzer and Mohandas 2022; Mohandas 2022). With these insights, Studies 10 and 11 emphasize the significance of clearly communicated expectations about the course design, ensuring that each stakeholder understands how to navigate between remote and face-to-face spaces to keep both parties engaged. Another suggestion from our studies is a proactive offer of easily accessible meeting spaces for students to keep them engaged at individual and team levels (Study 10). While acknowledging the unique hybrid characteristics of the HyFlex class, students and instructors must manage multiple modalities simultaneously and ensure easy switching from virtual to physical spaces and vice versa.

TECHNOLOGY-MEDIATED INTERACTIONS

Consistent with other literature, remote and face-to-face students occasionally struggle to grasp the components of effectively blending participation as they adapt to this emerging educational format. Our study with new instructors emphasizes that incorporating remote teammates and being a proficient remote participant requires intentional strategies, foundational skills for using the software and hardware employed in the class, and intentional discussions about the pros and cons of the participation modalities, including modeling the communication means by the instructor in large group sessions (Study 11). Although Study 9 reported that relatedness to the instructor was a statistically significant predictor of academic performance in a HyFlex model, it was also evident in Study 10 that not all instructors effectively created the most equitable experience for students while establishing instructor presence in the class. Mainly, the challenge arises when teamwork is not explicitly taught or scaffolded, and adding the HyFlex layer further complicates collaborative efforts. Study 8 calls for intentionally implementing teamwork strategies in HyFlex learning environments to address these complexities.

The role of instructors in HyFlex environments is multifaceted, with insights from Studies 3 and 10 shedding light on its crucial aspects. Mentzer and Mohandas (2022) brought attention to the need for face-to-face peers to actively engage their remote students and the occasional lack of remote students' contribution to group work, emphasizing the necessity of monitoring the engagement of all students and highlighting the need for instructors to assess and address students' participation levels actively. Study 10 also stressed instructors' varied approaches to establishing their presence across different modalities. While technology plays a pivotal role in leveraging presence and shaping the learning community, instructors displayed a variety of choices regarding technology use, attendance modality recommendations, and the autonomy granted to students. Two instructors preferred to use different technologies to establish and maintain their instructor preference with remote and face-to-face students; the third instructor offered technological alternatives mainly for remote students. Given the characteristics of HyFlex teaching, the onboarding process for instructors requires them to hone their skills, especially in managing the intricacies of technology and modality considerations (Study 11). It aligns with the broader theme across studies, highlighting the need for continuous training and adaptation to navigate the challenges associated with HyFlex teaching effectively.

IMPLICATIONS

One of the distinctive features highlighted by these studies is the flexibility and inclusivity embedded into HyFlex instructional design. Our studies emphasized how Interactive Synchronous HyFlex went beyond the limitations of a one-size-fits-all approach, offering students the autonomy to choose between face-to-face and remote attendance based on their individual preferences and circumstances and providing them with a digital version of course materials, recordings of each classroom session, and options for connecting with their peers and instructors. Several of our studies showed higher student BPN satisfaction in HyFlex courses compared to traditional face-to-face-only courses. The customized characteristics of HyFlex positions it as a potential exemplar of inclusive instructional design, recognizing that students have unique needs that may be better met through flexible and hybrid approaches.

REFERENCES

Akyol, Zehra, and D. Randy Garrison. 2008. "The Development of a Community of Inquiry over Time in an Online Course: Understanding the Progression and Integration of Social, Cognitive and Teaching Presence." *Online Learning* 12 (3–4). https://doi.org/10.24059/olj.v12i3-4.1680.

Akyol, Zehra, D. Randy Garrison, and M. Yasar Ozden. 2009. "Online and Blended Communities of Inquiry: Exploring the Developmental and Perceptional Differences." *The International Review of Research in Open and Distributed Learning* 10 (6): 65–83. https://doi.org/10.19173/irrodl.v10i6.765.

Banta, Trudy W., Jon P. Lund, Karen E. Black, and Frances W. Oblander. 1996. *Assessment in Practice: Putting Principles to Work on College Campuses*. Wiley.

Birjali, Marouane, Mohammed Kasri, and Abderrahim Beni-Hssane. 2021. "A Comprehensive Survey on Sentiment Analysis: Approaches, Challenges and Trends." *Knowledge-Based Systems* 226:107134. https://doi.org/10.1016/j.knosys.2021.107134.

Bozan, Karoly, James Gaskin, and Claire Stoner. 2024. "Student Engagement in the HyFlex and Online Classrooms: Lessons from the COVID-19 Pandemic." *Technology, Knowledge and Learning* 29 (1): 509–36. https://doi.org/10.1007/s10758-023-09661-x.

Calafiore, Pablo, and Emiliano Giudici. 2021. "Hybrid Versus HyFlex Instruction in an Introductory Finance Course." *International Journal of Education Research* 16 (1): 40–52.

Cohen, J. 1992. "A Power Primer." *Psychological Bulletin* 112 (1): 155–59.

Crocker, Amy F., and Susan N. Smith. 2019. "Person-First Language: Are We Practicing What We Preach?" *Journal of Multidisciplinary Healthcare* 12:125–29. https://doi.org/10.2147/JMDH.S140067.

Groves, J., L. R. Abts, and G. L. Goldberg. 2014. "Using an Engineering Design Process Portfolio Scoring Rubric to Structure Online High School Engineering Education." In *2014 ASEE Annual Conference & Exposition*. https://doi.org/10.18260/1-2-23254.

He, Wenliang, Daniel Gajski, George Farkas, and Mark Warschauer. 2015. "Implementing Flexible Hybrid Instruction in an Electrical Engineering Course: The Best of Three Worlds?" *Computers & Education* 81:59–68. https://doi.org/10.1016/j.compedu.2014.09.005.

Holzer, Julia, Marko Lüftenegger, Udo Käser, et al. 2021. "Students' Basic Needs and Well-Being During the COVID-19 Pandemic: A Two-Country Study of Basic Psychological Need Satisfaction, Intrinsic Learning Motivation, Positive Emotion and the Moderating Role of Self-Regulated Learning." *International Journal of Psychology* 56 (6): 843–52. https://doi.org/10.1002/ijop.12763.

Howell, Emily. 2022. "HyFlex Model of Higher Education: Understanding the Promise of Flexibility." *On the Horizon: The International Journal of Learning Futures* 30 (4): 173–81. https://doi.org/10.1108/OTH-04-2022-0019.

Israel, Glenn D. 1992. *Determining Sample Size*. Florida Cooperative Extension Service Fact Sheet PEOD-6. Institute of Food and Agricultural Sciences. University of Florida.

Kashif, Mahvish Fatima, and Rooha Shahid. 2021. "Students' Self-Regulation in Online Learning and Its Effect on Their Academic Achievement." *Global Educational Studies Review* 6 (3): 11–20. https://doi.org/10.31703/gesr.2021(VI-III).02.

Kohnke, Lucas, and Benjamin Luke Moorhouse. 2021. "Adopting HyFlex in Higher Education in Response to COVID-19: Students' Perspectives." *Open Learning: The Journal of Open, Distance and e-Learning* 36 (3): 231–44. https://doi.org/10.1080/02680513.2021.1906641.

Kohnke, Lucas, and Benjamin Luke Moorhouse. 2022. "Facilitating Synchronous Online Language Learning Through Zoom." *RELC Journal* 53 (1): 296–301. https://doi.org/10.1177/0033688220937235.

Lakens, Daniël, Anne M. Scheel, and Peder M. Isager. 2018. "Equivalence Testing for Psychological Research: A Tutorial." *Advances in Methods and Practices in Psychological Science* 1 (2): 259–69. https://doi.org/10.1177/2515245918770963.

Lakhal, Sawsen, Hager Khechine, and Daniel Pascot. 2014. "Academic Students' Satisfaction and Learning Outcomes in a HyFlex Course: Do Delivery Modes Matter?" In *Proceedings of World Conference on E-Learning*, edited by T. Bastiaens. Association for the Advancement of Computing in Education (AACE). https://www.learntechlib.org/primary/p/148994/.

Lightner, Constance A., and Carin A. Lightner-Laws. 2016. "A Blended Model: Simultaneously Teaching a Quantitative Course Traditionally, Online, and Remotely." *Interactive Learning Environments* 24 (1): 224–38. https://doi.org/10.1080/10494820.2013.841262.

Liu, Bing. 2022. *Sentiment Analysis: Mining Opinions, Sentiments, and Emotions*. Nota.

Love, Tyler S., Nicole Kreiser, Elsa Camargo, et al. 2015. "STEM Faculty Experiences with Students with Disabilities at a Land Grant Institution." *Journal of Education and Training Studies* 3 (1): 27–38.

Magana, Alejandra J., Tugba Karabiyik, Paul Thomas, Aparajita Jaiswal, Viranga Perera, and James Dworkin. 2022. "Teamwork Facilitation and Conflict Resolution Training in a HyFlex Course During the COVID-19 Pandemic." *Journal of Engineering Education* 111 (2): 446–73. https://doi.org/10.1002/jee.20450.

McDonald, Jason K., Jill Stefaniak, and Peter J. Rich. 2022. "Expecting the Unexpected: A Collaborative Autoethnography of Instructors' Experiences Teaching Advanced Instructional Design." *TechTrends* 66 (1): 90–101. https://doi.org/10.1007/s11528-021-00677-7.

Mentzer, Nathan, and Lakshmy Mohandas. 2022. "Student Experiences in an Interactive Synchronous HyFlex Design Thinking Course During COVID-19." *Interactive Learning Environments* 32 (5): 1613–28. https://doi.org/10.1080/10494820.2022.2124423.

Miller, Jackie B., Mark D. Risser, and Robert P. Griffiths. 2013. "Student Choice, Instructor Flexibility: Moving Beyond the Blended Instructional Model." *Issues and Trends in Educational Technology* 1 (1): 8–24. https://journals.uair.arizona.edu/index.php/itet/article/view/16464/16612.

Mohandas, Lakshmy, Nathan Mentzer, Adrie Koehler, and Shawn Farrington. 2023. "To Be Face-to-Face Today or to Be Remote Today: That Is the Question." In *Proceedings of the 2023 AERA Annual Meeting*. AERA. https://doi.org/10.3102/2017564.

Padilla Rodriguez, Brenda Cecilia. 2022. "The Rise and Fall of the HyFlex Approach in Mexico." *TechTrends* 66 (6): 911–13. https://doi.org/10.1007/s11528-022-00780-3.

Penrod, Jodie. 2022. "Staying Relevant: The Importance of Incorporating HyFlex Learning into Higher Education Strategy." *EDUCAUSE Review*, March 25. https://er.educause.edu/articles/2022/3/staying-relevant-the-importance-of-incorporating-hyflex-learning-into-higher-education-strategy.

Pfeifer, Mariel A., Eve Melanie Reiter, McKenna Hendrickson, and Julie Dangremond Stanton. 2020. "Speaking Up: A Model of Self-Advocacy for STEM Undergraduates with ADHD and/or Specific Learning Disabilities." *International Journal of STEM Education* 7 (33). https://doi.org/10.1186/s40594-020-00233-4.

Pintrich, Paul R. 1991. *A Manual for the Use of the Motivated Strategies for Learning Questionnaire (MSLQ)*. Technical Report No. 91-B-004. National Center for Research to Improve Postsecondary Teaching and Learning. https://files.eric.ed.gov/fulltext/ED338122.pdf.

Rasheed, Rasheed Abubakar, Amirrudin Kamsin, and Nor Aniza Abdullah. 2020. "Challenges in the Online Component of Blended Learning: A Systematic Review." *Computers & Education* 144 (January): 103701. https://doi.org/10.1016/j.compedu.2019.103701.

Rhoads, David D. 2020. "Traditional, Online or Both? A Comparative Study of University Student Learning and Satisfaction Between Traditional and Hyflex Delivery Modalities." EdD diss., Concordia University Irvine. https://www.proquest.com/dissertations-theses/traditional-online-both-comparative-study/docview/2410811261/se-2?accountid=13360.

Richardson, Jennifer C., Adrie A. Koehler, Erin D. Besser, Secil Caskurlu, JiEun Lim, and Chad M. Mueller. 2015. "Conceptualizing and Investigating Instructor Presence in Online Learning Environments." *The International Review of Research in Open and Distributed Learning* 16 (3). https://doi.org/10.19173/irrodl.v16i3.2123.

Schelly, Catherine L., Patricia L. Davies, and Craig L. Spooner. 2011. "Student Perceptions of Faculty Implementation of Universal Design for Learning." *Journal of Postsecondary Education and Disability* 24 (1): 17–30.

Wagner, Mary, Lynn Newman, Renee Cameto, Nicolle Garza, and Phyllis Levine. 2005. *After High School: A First Look at the Postschool Experiences of Youth with Disabilities. A Report from the National Longitudinal Transition Study-2 (NLTS2)*. Office of Special

Education Programs, US Department of Education. https://files.eric.ed.gov/fulltext/ED494935.pdf.

World Health Organization. 2023. "Statement on the Fifteenth Meeting of the IHR (2005) Emergency Committee on the COVID-19 Pandemic." May 5. https://www.who.int/news/item/05-05-2023-statement-on-the-fifteenth-meeting-of-the-international-health-regulations-(2005)-emergency-committee-regarding-the-coronavirus-disease-(covid-19)-pandemic.

York, Travis T., Charles Gibson, and Susan Rankin. 2015. "Defining and Measuring Academic Success." *Practical Assessment, Research, and Evaluation* 20 (5). https://doi.org/10.7275/hz5x-tx03.

6

TROUBLESHOOTING AND IMPROVING YOUR INTERACTIVE SYNCHRONOUS HYFLEX INSTRUCTION

Quality support can be a powerful catalyst for improving your teaching practice. Challenges often present valuable opportunities to learn, but continuously looking for ways to strengthen your skills over time is just as important. With that in mind, this chapter is divided into two parts: Part 1 explores what to do when you run into difficulties; part 2 offers strategies for intentionally refining and enhancing your teaching.

PART 1: WHAT TO DO WHEN YOU RUN INTO DIFFICULTY

When teaching an Interactive Synchronous HyFlex course, depending on how you set up your classroom, you may not have a sense of the modality mix you will have with your students until class time. On most days, attendance ratios

IMPROVING YOUR INTERACTIVE SYNCHRONOUS HYFLEX INSTRUCTION / 115

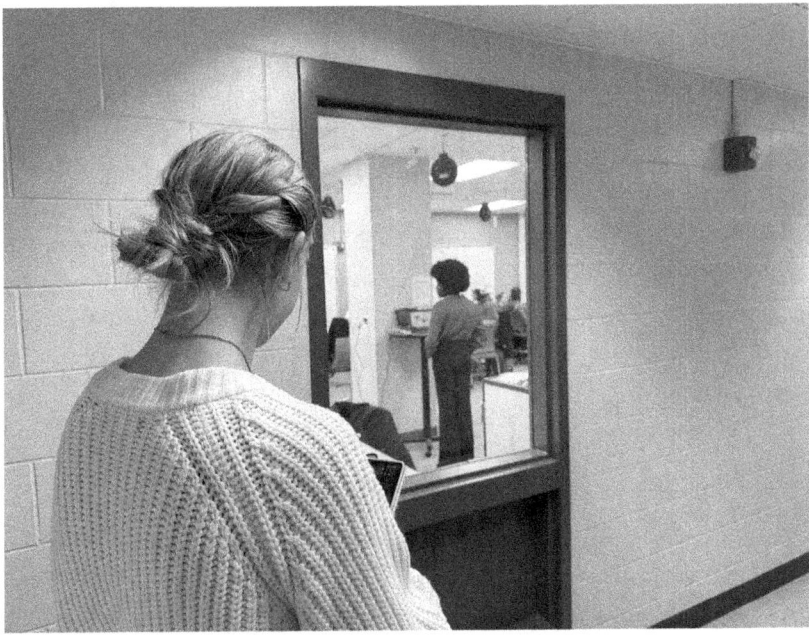

FIGURE 6.1 Observing other instructors is a great way to improve your own instruction. SOURCE: Abdul Moeed Asad (Co-author)

between face-to-face and remote students will remain consistent. However, there can be occasional variation due to external events such as semester breaks when students may like to extend their time at home or rough weather, or it can be for no apparent reason. Remember, just because someone is remote does not mean they are less engaged than students in the classroom. Your groups may be making progress, even if it seems invisible to you. However, in times where you feel your classroom dynamics are not working for you, consider the following strategies:

RELATED SECTION 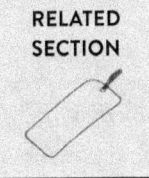	**Need More Insight into HyFlex-Specific Challenges?** Review the section "Anticipating Challenges" in chapter 2 to help you create expectations that work best to make your situation manageable.

COMMUNICATE WITH YOUR STUDENTS

When adjusting to HyFlex, communicate with your students about your intentions to make changes. Whether you're changing the attendance policy or how you conduct activities in the classroom, transparency can help get them on your side.

Similarly, ask for students' support when you encounter challenges. For instance, let them know if you will need to join class remotely while you are traveling and encourage students to rely on each other for help with technical issues. When you ask for help, students feel more comfortable chiming in with their expertise.

RENEW (INCLUSIVE) NORMS

While it may seem like a simple solution, reminding *all* students how to engage in the classroom can be effective in renewing classroom norms. Designing and facilitating learning experiences aligned with the Community of Inquiry can help create inclusive environments.

> **QUICK TIP**
>
> **How to Create Inclusive Norms**
>
> When renewing norms, unintentionally creating a culture where we privilege one modality over the other (usually face-to-face attendance over remote attendance) can easily happen. However, creating a welcoming environment helps to ensure that the classroom is inclusive. In HyFlex classrooms, reiterate and show that both remote and face-to-face attendance is equally appreciated.

Here are some ways to build student competencies:

- *Reiterate expectations:* Periodically (or as is necessary) review classroom expectations with all students. For instance, you might say, *If you plan to be remote in more than two consecutive sessions, you need to let me know. You can reach me on Teams or via email.* This will help remind students of the protocol to follow in case they would like to attend class remotely.

- *Practice together:* Implement practice sessions to help students get comfortable with hybrid interactions. Have everyone practice navigating the interface and joining their group's meeting. For example, say: *Everyone practice joining your group's channel. This is going to be something we do regularly when we have blended groups.* Keep in mind that some students likely will not have had prior blended experiences so you will need to review the procedures with them.
- *Model behavior:* Demonstrate inclusive behaviors as discussed in the chapter 4 section "Establish Your Presence to Build Rapport and Model Behavior". For instance, you can narrate your actions during class. While using the classroom collaboration software (e.g., Microsoft Teams), you can tell the class: *I am going to use [@channel name feature] so everyone gets a notification.* This helps students build competencies in how to use the software.

ASK FOR HELP

If you're running into problems in your HyFlex classroom, you can reach out to a more experienced colleague, a mentor, a department head, or even an online teaching community such as the HyFlex Learning Community (https://www.hyflexlearning.org/)—whomever or whatever you feel will be most helpful.

THE FINE PRINT

What to Do When You Face Technical Difficulties

While this text offers support for classroom management in Interactive Synchronous HyFlex courses, it cannot provide support for specific technical problems such as glitches that may exist or emerge with future hardware or software updates (your institution's IT department, however, is likely up for the task). That said, we want you to feel empowered to pause the conversation, acknowledge the issue, and take a brief moment to try to resolve it. Your students will understand, and although you will lose instruction time, dedicating time to resolving challenges emphasizes your priorities. For example, if the screen share feature stops working, taking steps to fix the issue reassures students that you value that everyone is able to follow along.

> **THE FINE PRINT**
>
>
>
> **What to Do When You Face Technical Difficulties**
> *(continued)*
>
> As we suggest above, you can recruit help when needed. You can ask your students or a teaching assistant (if one is available) to help with troubleshooting. If you find that the problem can't be solved quickly, the best path forward will align both with your teaching priorities (e.g., ensuring high-quality instruction) and your institution's guidelines (e.g., minimizing disruption to the schedule). Having backup or alternative methods ready is also important—although those are easiest to think through when you aren't in the middle of a crisis. Of course, occasionally the issue is too big to remedy in real time, and you might need to shift or reschedule. For example, if the internet goes down but you can still teach your face-to-face students, you could opt to record the session (with screen capturing software previously installed) for remote learners to watch later. However, if that same outage prevents critical activities for everyone, rescheduling could be best for all involved.

PART 2: IMPROVING YOUR HYFLEX INSTRUCTIONAL PRACTICE

As instructors, we are motivated to improve ourselves not only for ourselves but to create better learning experiences for our students. While we believe utilizing opportunities in your network can be beneficial (e.g., workshops/certifications offered by your institute), here we offer other HyFlex-specific opportunities that may be available to you.

USE RECORDINGS TO YOUR ADVANTAGE

Many of our instructors have found recordings to be invaluable resources for self-reflection. Recording class sessions can help you to (a) understand your pacing and the clarity of your delivery; (b) analyze your body language, tone of voice, and your engagement with all of your students (across modalities); (c) identify audio, video, or screen-sharing problems; and (d) consider the effectiveness of specific instructional strategies for all students

A level of self-monitoring is useful because our students can be too polite to point out obvious technical issues such as poor audio.

OBSERVE OTHER HYFLEX INSTRUCTORS

Our default assumption is that every instructor is able to run a HyFlex classroom. However, observing how more experienced instructors teach their classes is a good idea (see figure 6.1). Watching an effective HyFlex instructor use technology in their classroom and engage with students can be inspiring.

ASK YOUR STUDENTS

Periodically ask for feedback from your students so that you may understand their experiences and identify areas for improvement related to remote participation, face-to-face participation, and blending the two modalities in their small groups. You can use quick surveys or informal discussions for this purpose. An example survey question could be *On a scale of 1–5, how comfortable are you blending peers in the room and online?* An open discussion could start with *What's working well so far? Where are you still getting stuck?* Listen for recurring problems (e.g., remote students not feeling heard) and address them promptly.

ASK FOR A SECOND OPINION

In an Interactive Synchronous HyFlex classroom, favoring either remote or face-to-face students can happen easily, even when you are actively trying to engage both modalities equally. Consider inviting a colleague, friend, or someone from an instructional excellence unit in your university to observe your classroom, and ask them to help you evaluate how you are engaging with the classroom. An observer can share insights into areas that might have become your blind spots. Additionally, outside observers can highlight areas where you excel. Importantly, they can share new ideas and approaches that you may not have considered so far.

EXPERIMENT!

Gradually introduce new tools or technology to your classroom and observe the effect they have. In terms of tools, you could try advanced polling platforms (e.g., Mentimeter, Kahoot!), collaborative whiteboards (e.g., Miro, FigJam), or other course-specific tool (e.g., Figma for design). Better hardware like an external microphone or headset could improve the remote students' experience.

CONCLUSION

Our experience and research shows that the Interactive Synchronous HyFlex format makes classrooms more inclusive and accessible for students (as shown in figure C.1). Adopting Interactive Synchronous HyFlex can make classroom management more complex, but we hope that the experience we have offered in this book helps you to smoothly transition (chapter 2), successfully run (chapter 3), and troubleshoot your HyFlex classroom (chapter 6). Additionally, we hope we have shown that Interactive Synchronous HyFlex can transfer well outside of medium-sized active learning classrooms to other contexts (chapter 4).

KEY TAKEAWAYS

As you make Interactive Synchronous HyFlex your own, the following are some key lessons to take away from our work.

SETTING CLEAR EXPECTATIONS

One thing we reiterate is to create clear expectations and to reestablish them however often you need to. Your expectations include how you want students to show up to the classroom (i.e., your policy on remote attendance) and how you'd like them to participate (e.g., raising their hands on Microsoft Teams or Zoom and ensuring students are heard). If you need help with creating and

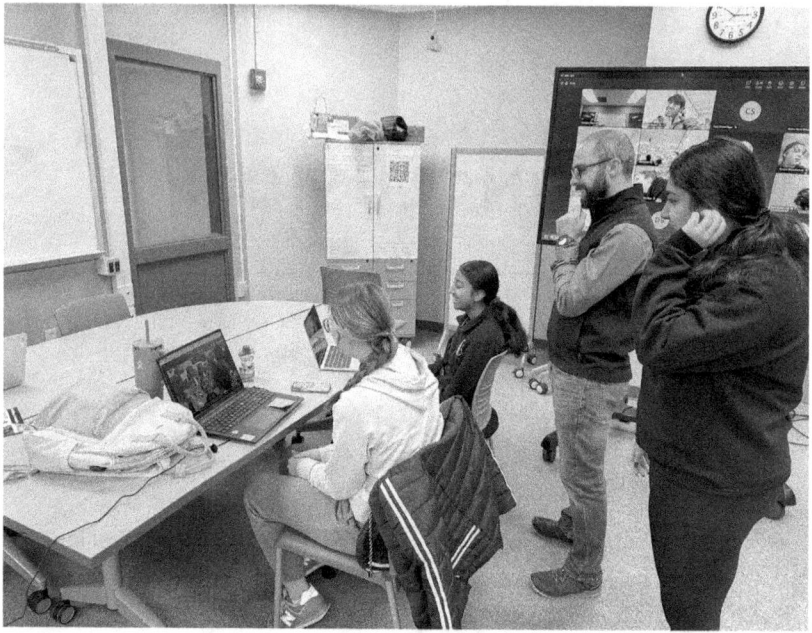

FIGURE C.1 Instructor flexibility to adopt Interactive Synchronous HyFlex teaching can make the classroom more accessible to students. SOURCE: Abdul Moeed Asad (Co-author)

communicating your expectations, revisit chapter 2. Sometimes clarity comes from repetition: You may want to repeat your expectations every so often to the class to ensure that everyone understands them and knows they are meant to be followed. Importantly, if you see that your norms are not working, feel empowered to modify them and communicate this to your students.

ESTABLISH AN INCLUSIVE AND ENGAGING CULTURE

As instructors, we play an important role in establishing an inclusive culture that equally values remote and face-to-face participation. If students feel seen and heard, they will participate, regardless of their modality. However, if the rare student does not engage, we can coach students to take accountability for their learning (e.g., confronting them with how they choose to engage by asking them if it's working for them and why).

Generally, instructors accustomed to teaching face-to-face courses need to pay special attention to remote students. Remote students feel ignored if their voice is not included in the classroom discussion and may therefore disengage. Emphasizing their importance with your words and actions can help face-to-face students recognize the importance of facilitating remote students' participation to ensure an inclusive culture.

After a little practice, we are confident that you and your students will be able to create an inclusive classroom culture.

LEVERAGE TECHNOLOGIES THAT FACILITATE INTERACTION ACROSS MODALITIES

In your classroom, we recommend devising activities that are digital-first so that they are inclusive of both remote and face-to-face students.

We encourage instructors to think about how going digital-first may have additional benefits that go beyond their physical counterparts. Beyond being more inclusive, normal classroom activities such as classroom discussion and presentations can be made more dynamic by using technology in the classroom (as shown in figure C.2). Experiment with introducing technology in the classroom. Here are some suggestions:

FIGURE C.2 Students are collaborating over their work across modalities. SOURCE: Abdul Moeed Asad (Co-author)

- Interactive presentation software such as Mentimeter can help put student responses front and center in the classroom for further discussion.
- Digital polls are easy to manage and often come with built-in videoconferencing software. Specialized polling solutions can add more fun (e.g., Kahoot!) because of their gamification features.
- Discussions can be meaningfully archived in the form of threads, letting the class use them as a resource (e.g., for an assignment that has students respond to feedback).

To ensure the smooth integration of technologies, provide students with opportunities to practice with the technologies you plan to use to avoid technical issues during and after class time. Understand that the teaching staff (or their support staff) will have to spend some time helping students troubleshoot technical issues throughout the term. Understanding the affordances of both HyFlex and selected technologies will help you to make the best decisions for your given context. For instance, using Microsoft Teams to facilitate class sessions allows students and the instructor to easily associate with each other, recordings and chats persist after the session has ended, and notifications within the system offer ways for students and the instructor to observe each other's behavior and thus to see how everyone is navigating within the learning environment.

KEEP ON IMPROVING

We're sure you've heard this before, but as with most things, you will improve your implementation of HyFlex iteratively. If you feel your first attempts were not as successful as you would have liked, we are certain that by embracing a mindset of continuous improvement and remaining responsive to student needs, you will be able to improve your practice and provide a more accessible environment for your students.

FINAL THOUGHTS

Implementing HyFlex is not without its challenges, but the potential rewards make it a worthwhile endeavor. Interactive Synchronous HyFlex represents a significant step forward in educational practice, directly addressing the evolving needs identified in the publication *2022 Students and Technology Report* EDUCAUSE report (Robert 2022). As the research indicates, students are seeking educational experiences that balance flexibility, social interaction, and academic engagement—regardless of modality. Interactive Synchronous HyFlex learning environments inherently support these priorities by allowing students to choose their mode of participation while maintaining a cohesive learning community and interactions.

Furthermore, the collaborative technologies integral to HyFlex design, such as screen sharing, live captioning, and interactive digital workspaces, provide the assistive features that the research shows benefit all students, not just those with documented disabilities. By incorporating these inclusive technologies, HyFlex classrooms address the equity concerns highlighted in the EDUCAUSE report, particularly regarding device access and technological challenges that impact student wellness.

According to the World Economic Forum (2021) survey, EDUCAUSE Horizon report, McKinsey Global survey (Galvin and LaBerge 2021), and Inside Higher Ed, higher education in the future is indeed becoming a hybrid of in-person and remote learning, with HyFlex emerging as the new norm in education. The journey of implementing and refining HyFlex learning is an ongoing process, but with a commitment to continuous improvement, the benefits for both students and educators are significant—creating learning environments that are more accessible and inclusive.

REFERENCES

Bradoo, Gaurav. 2025. "Seamless Scalable Smart Streamlining HyFlex Learning." *EDUCAUSE Review*, March 10. https://er.educause.edu/articles/sponsored/2025/3/seamless-scalable-smart-streamlining-hyflex-learning

Galvin, Jeff, and Laura LaBerge. 2021. "Digital Strategy in the Postpandemic Era." May 21. McKinsey. https://www.mckinsey.com/capabilities/mckinsey-digital/our-insights/the-new-digital-edge-rethinking-strategy-for-the-postpandemic-era

Robert, Jenay. 2022. *2022 Students and Technology Report: Rebalancing the Student Experience*. EDUCAUSE. https://library.educause.edu/resources/2022/10/2022-students-and-technology-report-rebalancing-the-student-experience

World Economic Forum. 2021. *Global Risks Report 2021*. https://www.weforum.org/publications/the-global-risks-report-2021/

ABOUT THE AUTHORS

NATHAN MENTZER is a professor of technology and engineering education at Purdue University, where his primary focus is preparing future teachers for the classroom. He has more than twenty years of experience as an educator in the secondary and postsecondary public school systems. He is recognized by the International Technology and Engineering Educators Association (ITEEA) as a Distinguished Technology Educator and National Teacher Effectiveness Coach. With National Science Foundation grant funding, Mentzer's team has published sixteen papers related to HyFlex and received nine awards for their work related to the topic, including the QS Reimagine Education North America Gold Award.

ABDUL MOEED ASAD is a research assistant at Purdue University, focused on improving design education. He began using the Interactive Synchronous HyFlex model after struggling to engage online students while teaching design courses. This book stems from Asad's experiences implementing this innovative pedagogical approach. Today, he champions HyFlex as a new standard that expands possibilities beyond traditional face-to-face instruction.

ADRIE A. KOEHLER is an associate professor in the Learning Design and Technology program in Purdue's College of Education, where she focuses on preparing undergraduate and graduate students to design educational experiences in blended and online environments. Prior to pursuing a career in higher education, she worked as a high school business teacher. Koehler is using what she has learned from implementing, observing, and researching the Interactive Synchronous HyFlex model to prepare preservice instructors for the realities they will encounter in the classroom.

LAKSHMY MOHANDAS is a software design lecturer in EPICS, a service-learning design program at Purdue University, where she focuses on developing innovative teaching methodologies and experiential learning experiences. With a background in EdTech and instructional design, she pioneered the

Interactive Synchronous HyFlex model, resuming face-to-face instruction in the summer of 2020, which became the foundation for our QS Reimagine Education North America Gold Award. For Mohandas, HyFlex is not simply an alternative teaching mode—it is also a transformational educational tool that ensures no student ever has to miss an opportunity to learn and collaborate, regardless of their physical location or circumstances.

ELNARA MAMMADOVA is a PhD candidate in technology at Purdue Polytechnic. As a former special educator, her research focuses on advancing digital accessibility for undergraduate students with disabilities enrolled in STEM courses. She leverages learning analytics to inform curriculum development and lesson planning, particularly in Interactive Synchronous HyFlex teaching and learning settings. By analyzing students' learning experiences and instructional strategies, Mammadova aims to create data-driven strategies for designing digitally accessible course materials and lessons.

www.ingramcontent.com/pod-product-compliance
Lightning Source LLC
Chambersburg PA
CBHW070403240426
43661CB00056B/2517